BOSS GARDENER
The Life and Times of John McLaren

BOSS GARDENER
The Life and Times of John McLaren
Tom Girvan Aikman

Don't Call It Frisco Press

Published by Don't Call It Frisco Press.

Edited by Laurie Cohn.

Design and Layout by Barbara Luck.

Cover portrait by Richard Sigberman.

Set in 11 point Century Old Style. Reproduced from pages generated on the Macintosh II computer and printed on the Apple LaserWriter printer.

ISBN 0-917583-18-3

Printed in the United States of America.

PHOTO CREDITS

Robin Lew: 68

National Maritime Museum, San Francisco: 28, 34, 36

Photography Center, San Francisco Recreation and Park Department: 76
San Mateo County Historical Association: 41-44

All other photos are courtesy of the following:

Mr. James C. Aikman
Mr. Raymond H. Clary
McLaren Lodge
Mrs. Maridu McLeod
Mrs. Martha Smith

For
C. W. M. A.
and
J. C. A.,
E. J. M. A.

Foreword

As a child growing up, my sister, brothers, and I heard two names mentioned almost daily in our home—Hamish MacGregor and John McLaren. The two were related, their mothers being cousins.

The Rev. Dr. James MacGregor, minister of St. Cuthbert's, Edinburgh, was a Moderator of the General Assembly of the Church of Scotland, a Chaplain to Queen Victoria, and the friend of Disraeli and the Duke of Argyll. Many years ago, in 1912, Lady Frances Balfour wrote his biography. MacGregor's mother was Margaret McDougall of Artalnaig in the Parish of Kenmore in Perthshire.

John McLaren, the other oft-quoted name, was my grandmother's oldest brother and a Scottish gardener who carved for himself an unforgettable name as the creator of Golden Gate Park in San Francisco. His mother was Catherine Walker McDougall, also from Artalnaig, and she was Margaret McDougall's cousin.

Much has been written, and in many places, of McLaren's horticultural career, rather less of his family background, Scottish boyhood, and personal life. With my particular genes, I thought I might try to make good the lack. In telling the story as it was told to me by my mother and grandmother, and as I have come to know it over the years, I received much help and therefore must make appropriate acknowledgement.

I wish, first, to thank Mrs. Maridhu McLeod of San Anselmo, California, for her kindness in giving me unrestricted access to her father's notes. Her father,

*Catherine Walker McDougall Aikman,
McLaren's niece.*

the late Mr. Owen Holmes, was the husband of Jean Finlayson, John McLaren's god-daughter. He and McLaren were planning a biography when the Second World War broke out. Because of the War, the work was never started but Mrs. McLeod preserved her father's notes and I am grateful to her for making them so readily available to me. I thank her also for providing the photographs of her mother.

I also wish to thank the San Mateo County Historical Association for the information they provided so willingly upon request, information which was invaluable to me when writing of John McLaren's San Mateo years.

Ms. Susan Karasz, Assistant to the Director of the Massachusetts Horticultural Society, furnished me with the information I requested with regard to the George Robert White Medal and certainly must be thanked for her ready and charming assistance.

My obligation to Mr. Raymond H. Clary's two excellent volumes on Golden Gate Park is gratefully acknowledged in footnotes but I thank him also for providing several photographs and for answering questions.

My sister, Mrs. Margaret MacLaren of Scotland, spent many hours in family research and I thank her for doing so and for reminding me of several important facts which I had forgotten.

Special thanks is expressed to my cousin, Mrs. Martha McLaren Daniels, John McLaren's great-granddaughter, for writing the Introduction. Based upon her childhood memories, it is extremely well done and adds greatly to the picture. She also provided several family photographs for which I thank her—and also for saving me from a number of mistakes!

Mrs. Laraine Mallon of Poughkeepsie, New York, my secretary and Mrs. Melba Hippauf, also of Poughkeepsie, must be thanked for typing the manuscript.

Finally, my gratitude to Eiluned, my wife, for her unfailing support in all things but especially for displaying a patience greater than Job's while I was writing my story.

Tom Girvan Aikman
Pleasant Valley, N.Y.
March, 1988

Contents

Introduction

My mother Matie, Martha McLaren Daniels, who was John McLaren's granddaughter, once said that her grandfather's landscape expressed the vigorous and somber spirit of Highland poetry. I was able to visit the country around Stirling where John McLaren was born, to meet my Scottish cousins, and to travel north into the Highlands when my husband held an exchange professorship at Glasgow University in 1978. At the fruit stands and the fishmongers' shops on Dumbarton Road, Glasgow, and returning by bus from Loch Lomond on Sunday afternoons, I recognized the sturdy Scottish spirit my mother told me of. We always used public transportation while touring Scotland, and I heard sometimes on return trips the same tunes I heard as a child sitting at the top of my bedroom door when the Robert Burns Society of San Francisco met in the Park Lodge.

My Stirling cousins, the Aikmans, showed us the beautiful countryside of McLaren's youth and even took us to a house thought to have been his childhood residence. It was quite different from the photograph of the single-story stone house which my mother thought his birthplace. I nonetheless knocked at the door of the two-story dwelling on a slight hill, not far from Stirling, and introduced myself to a gracious older woman who showed me through the numerous small and pleasant rooms. The possibility that McLaren had lived there before having gone off to America delighted her. He was a legendary figure.

In order to write this profile, my cousin the Reverend Tom Aikman, whose maternal grandmother was my great-grandfather's sister, has not only travelled several times from his home in New York State to consult San Francisco archives and review family records and photographs, but has gone through innumerable newspaper articles. Even now, almost fifty years since my great-grandfather's death, I receive occasional newspaper clippings. The slightest excuse still inspires bursts of nostalgia sending journalists back to their typewriters to marvel at the man who built Golden Gate Park on sand dunes.

John McLaren and the San Francisco parks had a long, successful relationship, although he had no taste for rhetoric or fanfare, and the newsmen at first considered the building of the Park somewhat comic. The prevailing opinion when the first work began on those one thousand acres of sand exposed every summer afternoon to winds blowing at a rate of twenty to thirty miles per hour was that "we have a white elephant on our hands." Only when those acres gradually came to equal and then to exceed in splendor Boston's Public Gardens, Central Park in New York, and even many of the great European parks, did the newspapers follow its development attentively. The Park and its creator had captured the imagination of the city. Those miles of parkland, jewelled with lakes and waterfalls, required, even in a technologically efficient society, consistent human attention, well-trained labor, and substantial sums of money. McLaren accepted, even encouraged, the adulation of San Francisco citizens in order to project his Victorian dream into the twentieth century. He was preoccupied with Golden Gate Park, to the exclusion, my mother thought, of almost everything else in his life.

The visitor to the Park normally tackles first the main thoroughfare leading to the public buildings and amusements—the aquarium, museum, conservatory, and Japanese Tea Garden. Prominent in this public area are statues of the great, among them the poet Robert Burns, and, of course, numerous California civic leaders, especially those having made substantial financial contributions to the Park's development. Only a visitor searching for it will find in a simply landscaped dell a short stocky figure gazing reflectively at his palmful of seeds. My six foot son David's first response was, "Mom, he was so small." And so I remember him when I was a young child. To my child's eye he was small and serene.

My mother lived in Golden Gate Park Lodge with her grandfather until her marriage in 1932. There were few of the McLaren family in this country. The two were close because of this, but also because they shared an artistic nature. McLaren expressed his in a romantic naturalism in the design of his gardens. My mother was a modernist and a painter of abstract canvases. While viewing nature from quite different perspectives, they shared with equal, perhaps obsessive, intensity a pursuit of their creative aims.

My two brothers and I were born within three years, in McLaren's nineties, immediately preceding the second World War. Because of his pleasure in us and my mother's understandable appreciation of his support with her young family, the Lodge was our second home between 1935 and 1943. In 1942, my father had finally determined to sell his successful dairy farm in Marin County, California, and to join as an enlisted man his naval officer brother and cousins. In 1943, my mother, with the assistance of many good family friends and the Lodge's household staff, presided over the closing of her family residence. When she closed the Lodge's front door in 1943 she also took leave of her position, always a central one, in John McLaren's vital and sustaining constellation.

We children were immersed in this McLaren ambiance in our very early years. While at the Lodge we were wrapped in Victorian well-being and concern. We were nursed through whooping cough, mumps, and measles by Maggie Miller, earlier my mother's nursemaid and now the Lodge's housekeeper. All the extended household, including my great-grandfather's formidably efficient nurse Agnes Ebeling and the gentle cook Mary scrutinized and supervised us, assisting my mother with our early training. At all times, the Victorian order of the household was maintained: silver shone, mahogany gleamed, carpet, upholstery, and draperies were maintained as the country slipped into world war. Black-out curtains were added to the Victorian draperies when Pearl Harbor was bombed in December 1941. I recall that in addition to the heavily draped windows, there was in the spacious doorways between rooms floor-length, wine-colored velvet stuff in which we hid to escape dosages of cod liver oil. I remember being led through my great-grandmother's bedroom, unoccupied for fifteen years after her death, but still pulsing with Victorian propriety. I was allowed to observe the objects on Jane McLaren's dressing table, to hold her heavy silver hairbrush decorated with roses, to peek into her jewelry box, sometimes to touch the golden locket on which a long-haired water nymph blew diamond soap bubbles. In the window seat from which Mrs. McLaren saw guests come up the Lodge's driveway was the sewing box which I have used the past thirty years. Jane McLaren told her granddaughter that little girls should not turn "cart wheels," especially not on Sundays, when quiet conversation, knitting, or sewing were appropriate pastimes.

A place of special calm in the anxious early-war years was Grandpa McLaren's office, where he had for decades planned and supervised the Park's development and maintenance. While the household prepared for the dinner hour, we visited with him there so as not to interfere with the exacting requirements of the evening meal, pinnacle of 19th-century daily ritual. In contrast to the living quarters of the Lodge, the office had the aura of a work place: it was small and sunny, the desk cluttered with books and papers. My great-grandfather sat in his swivel chair, fully dressed for business affairs in a three-piece tweed suit—scratchy, I remember, to my bare legs when I sat in his otherwise most comfortable lap. It was not usually I who had that cozy position in his lap, but my brother John McLaren Daniels, while the youngest of us, Ralph Chandler Daniels III, played at his feet. Being the eldest and most agile, I was able to scramble up to the desk top from which I could observe my old Grandpa and see the gleam of his watch chain crossing his stomach. He and I exchanged steady gazes. It was very comfortable at the end of a long day to be there with him in that warm, simply furnished room   The smell of the cigars stored in the interestingly decorated box on the desk top was pleasant too.   It was sometimes at the top of the stairway outside his bedroom door that we unlaced our great-grandfather's boot, but often it was there in his office that we three worked together at his feet in that demanding task of freeing him from all those criss-crossed laces for his evening slippers. We knew this to be important work which we could do best. In one pocket Grandpa had many shiny dimes and in another sweet hoarhound drops. From one or both of those pockets he would slowly and deliberately draw forth our rewards. His hands, so intimately known as he dispensed our wages, I remember with special affection. They were muscular with rather short fingers, as were the hands of my dairy farmer father. They seemed large to me, but perhaps hands which have accomplished a great deal can appear large to a small child.

I am grateful to my cousin Tom for having revived these sustaining memories. With arduous research he has been able to set in order the facts of my great-grandfather's long and distinguished life as a master gardener. He has also sensitively interpreted McLaren's relationships to those with whom he lived and worked. While acknowledging the largeness of his dreams and vision, Tom does not allow the man to slip off into the world of legend. I am able to recognize him as the Grandpa with whom I visited so pleasantly before supper.

Martha McLaren Daniels

1   The Highland Parents

In the Royal Burgh of Stirling, Scotland—beneath the shadow of the ancient and historic Castle where as a boy James VI, son of Mary, Queen of Scots, had his ears boxed by George Buchanan, his Erasmian tutor—there stands the Church of the Holy Rude. A long, steep street winds up to it—Spittal Street, named for Robert Spittal, tailor to King James IV. The Church, a noble structure, has some claim to fame if only because James VI was crowned there and John Knox, firebrand of the Scottish Reformation, once "wagged his heid" in its pulpit.

In the cemetery behind the church, cold and grey, stands a chaste and durable headstone with the simple inscription:

In
Loving Memory of
DONALD MCLAREN
who died 19th June, 1902,
Aged 87 years,
And CATHERINE MCDOUGALL, his wife,
who died 25th April, 1905,
Aged 87 years.

The names are those of the father and mother of John McLaren of Golden Gate Park, San Francisco, one of a host of frustrated, restless young men, adventuresome, brainy, and idealistic (in a pragmatic kind of way) who, because of economic hardship and hampering circumstances, left their native heath to seek fame and fortune abroad in the outposts of the

Empire. Some went to Canada, some to Australia, some to New Zealand, some to South Africa, and some to other places. But wherever they went, they carried with them their Scottish character, their Scottish tongue, and their (sometimes) outsized Scottish dreams.

> Come ye home a hero
> Or come not home at all.

Originally, the young John McLaren had thought to go to India, the "Jewel in the Crown," but his mother somehow managed to induce him to change his mind and in the end he chose America, the New World, the "Golden West," if only because the opportunity came one afternoon in Edinburgh through Mr. George Howard, an American gentleman from San Mateo, out in California. It was in America, in San Francisco's Golden Gate Park, that McLaren made his name.

In Barrie's "Dear Brutus," Lob, the gardener, "even grew hats." John McLaren couldn't grow hats but he could grow trees—two million of them (and from seed) in the San Mateo/San Francisco area alone—and in places where no one else had been able to grow trees before. The cynics scoffed, saying that it couldn't be done but "There is always a way," as Wodehouse's Jeeves used to say and John McLaren found it.

Donald McLaren and Catherine Walker McDougall, John's parents, were Gaelic-speaking highlanders from Artalnaig on the south side of Loch Tay, deep in the Perthshire Highlands. Far back, the McDougalls had come south from Oban in Argyll, the heart of Tir-nam-Beann (pronounced Tjeer-nam-Ben, "Land of the Hills," i.e. The Highlands). There were farmers mostly. Sheep farmers.

Catherine was intensely proud of her clan's sturdy story. Centuries before she was born, the chief of the clan had engaged Robert Bruce in hand-to-hand combat. The Bruce had entertained bandit designs on

Artalnaig, Perthshire.

the McDougall territory and the McDougall, resenting the intrusion, decided to do something about it. He confronted the future king somewhere near the Pass of Brander and, in the duel that followed, Bruce took to his heels and ran but not before the McDougall had grabbed the brooch from his doublet. Thus did the "Bruce Brooch" become the property of the Clan McDougall and is still today the pride of all Dunollie and in the custody, presumably, of the Maid of Lorne, the present chief, whose home is in Benderloch, that wild but beautiful stretch of Gaeldom lying to the north of Connel, the ancient home of Ossian's Deirdre—"Deirdre of the Sorrows."

> There has been again no woman born
> Who was so beautiful....

Catherine Walker McDougall was the child of John McDougall, who married Catherine McNab of Killin in 1809. John, like Donald his father, was a sheep farmer. Catherine (John of Golden Gate's

Loch Tay (from Artalnaig).

mother) was born in 1818, just after Waterloo, one of history's decisive battles, when James Monroe was president of the United States. She was born at Balmoich, a place of overpowering beauty, where Ben Lawers' gently sweeping peak, on a summer's day, may be seen reflected in the loch as in a mirror. The Ben (hill in English) is supremely beautiful—almost, some would say, divine.

When Catherine was in her teens, a young shepherd, Donald McLaren, came to work on her father's farm and the two fell in love. It was a love which seemed predestined, although Monod might disagree ("Chance alone is at the source of innovation.") It was also a love whose course did not run smoothly. At least, not to start with. It is a common story. Relations in the home were strained. Catherine's parents felt their pride had been wounded and were disappointed that their daughter should be "marrying one beneath her station," as they put it. They did what they could to end the liaison, even sending Catherine to Callander, a distant town, for a time, hoping thereby to forestall a wedding. But all to no avail. Catherine's love ran deep. "If ever I am to marry," she said in the Gaelic, "it is to Donald McLaren I will marry." And marry her Donald she did—in Comrie Parish, on February 6, 1846, happily, with her parents' blessing.

Donald and Catherine McLaren were married for more than fifty years and it was an ideal union. "Others may have married richer men, or handsomer men," Catherine used to say to her granddaughter (my mother), "but I married the best man and the best husband."

Donald McLaren, the shepherd, was a quiet man, gentle and devout and with the soft blue eyes of the Gael. Catherine, on the other hand, could be haughty and self-willed, was highly intelligent, house-proud, and extremely practical. Opposites who matched. "Made for each other," as their daughter (my grandmother) used to say and they created a happy home for their children, giving them security, moral stability, and Calvinistic discipline—what Bonhoeffer called *Zucht*.

Donald and Catherine set up their first home at Craigford, near Whins-of-Milton, in Stirlingshire. The house still stands, a Georgian structure of slate and stone with two or three acres of land and a barn or two. There, the couple had five children, more than they could really afford. John, the oldest, was born, with snow flurries flying, on Sunday December 20, 1846. Three years later, he was followed by Dugald, Duncan, and then Margaret, the only girl (my grandmother). Fifth and last came Peter who was born in September 1857 and died young.

Dugald was an astute businessman, a grocer, who worked incredibly hard and eventually owned several grocery stores down in England, in Lancashire ("Cottonopolis"). He ended up quite prosperous. Margaret married Tom Girvan, a tall, well-set-up, but rather unreliable character whom I never knew, with whom she eventually took over the old home and farm.

At Craigford, Donald the shepherd set up as a market-gardener and managed to make an adequate, if sometimes, precarious, living. When John was five years old he was enrolled in a school in Whins-of-Milton, the fee being sixpence per month. He received the normal education of the day, the schooling being sound, if limited. Teachers knew their job and could open imagination's doors. Discipline, a seemingly lost art in today's world of "progressive" education, was firm and pupils had to toe the line or face the consequences (i.e. the "belt.")

Children walked to school, unlike today when they are driven by bus. Children see little being driven to school in a bus. They miss the wonders of the hedgerow. Young John had to foot it, whatever the weather, crossing on the way, a small, wooden bridge over the Bannock, all the time observing the wonders of Nature. Years later, John Stanton, the San Francisco artist, painted a picture of the bridge which hung in McLaren's home at the Lodge on Stanyan Street in San Francisco next to Keith's "Scottish Glen." The "Glen" and the "Wee Brig," as he called it, were among his most treasured possessions. They pictorialized his boyhood memories.

At school, young John learned something of history, geography, grammar, spelling, and the "sums." He was not academic, but was no slouch either. He was an average pupil who did moderately well and was happy. He never attended high school, much less a university, but the day was to come when he would receive an honorary Doctorate of Laws (LL.D) and further honors from prestigious places. A five hundred acre park and a rhododendron would one day be given his name. An annual "John McLaren Day" would be proclaimed by the Mayor of San Francisco and a best-selling and erudite work on gardening, now out of print, would be authored by him. (Those fortunate enough to own a copy have a collector's piece on their hands.) The day would also come when his statue would be placed in Golden Gate

Craigford, McLaren's birthplace.

Park, and he would become the friend and confidant
of many of the world's famous—Harry Lauder, Sir
Thomas Lipton, Enrico Caruso, John Muir, Jack
London, Jackie Coogan, and dozens more. When he
died, his body lay in state, thousands filing past in
tribute and respect.

John McLaren was short and thick-set, like his
father in looks, with shrewd, grey, searching eyes and
his mother's artistic nature. His mother's fierce
independence was also stamped on his birth certificate.
As the oldest child, he had responsibility for the
younger siblings, and his chores to see to before and
after school—feeding the calves, carrying in coals,
collecting the eggs, running messages to Milton Mill
and the Whins. He particularly liked working in the
garden. "I think I was born with the gift of being able
to make things grow," he used to say in later life. For

doing his chores he received not a penny. Children were members of a family and, as such, were taught to share in the duties and responsibilities as well as enjoy the benefits and privileges of corporate family life. He loved the out-of-doors, the woods and the fields, the hills and the burn, the smell of the hay and the clover. He grew up with a love of Nature as intense and ardent as Loren Eisley's. It was Nature and not humanity which inspired his faith.

Even as a boy, John McLaren had extraordinary powers of observation and an amazing grasp of the ways of Nature. One day the schoolmaster discovered him gazing over the schoolhouse wall and when asked why, the boy replied, "Please Sir, your flowers'll no' grow. They're too close to the dyke and can't see the sun." He was engaged immediately as the school's official gardener!

He also kept rabbits, as country boys do, but here too, he was a bold exception. Most boys imprison them in a hutch or a cage. Young John scratched out underground tunnels to enable them to live in their natural habitat.

Craigford was a happy home.   Life was wholesome and clean and not infrequently Spartan. The children were taught solid virtues—honesty, respect, reverence, thrift, hard work, and the clear-cut difference between what is right and what is wrong. Loyalty to one another was an article of faith. "Always be true to each other," was a constant injunction. And they were taught too, never to be useless. "Don't eat of the bread of idleness." It was a home where, if there was punishment, it was administered as an expression of love. These, and other values were implanted in them from childhood, a parental legacy which was to influence the course of their lives.

There was nothing romantic about the life. There were setbacks and hardships and the McLarens were poor.   They ate a lot of "skirlie" (a proletarian concoction of oatmeal and onions, fried in roast

Margaret McLaren Girvan, McLaren's only sister.

dripping—tasty and filling). But they were no poorer than their neighbors and they never felt poor. Like Lamb's Captain Jackson, they had "nothing to live on but seemed to live on everything."

The late Principal David Cairns, a Moderator of the General Assembly of the Church of Scotland, once wrote: "Of all the many good gifts God has given me, among the greatest I would put my father and mother and the home they made for us, their children. I am not at all blind to the limitations and even faults, but they both, in different ways, made it easier for us to believe in goodness and in God." A noble tribute and one which might well have been paid by John McLaren to his highland parents.

My great-grandparents left Craigford in 1857 or 1858, having rented Muirside, a small farm nearby. Muirside was to be their home for the rest of their lives. In later years, John, grateful for all they had done for himself, his brothers, and sister, purchased Muirside as a gift for his parents and it remained in the family until sold by my parents in 1935. His younger brother, Dugald, travelled north from Wittington, his home in Lancashire, to bid at the auction on his behalf. Next day, their mother wrote to tell of the purchase. The following is part of her letter.

Muirside
January 27th. 1897

Dear Son and Daughter,

It is with great pleasure I begin to write to acquaint you of the joyful news that you are laird and lady of Muirside. The sale came off yesterday. It was a sore battle but Dugald won. It was struck down at the handsome sum of five hundred and forty five pounds, very cheap....We lost the Rattray's gardens. John Waterston, our worthy neighbor, bought them. Dugald came on Wednesday. He did not come back the night of the sale as they are very busy just now. When your father came home, I did not know him at first. He looked so proud. Dugald sent a cab home with him. The farmers around us were all very glad you got it. They came in to see us. They drank to your health and wish you both great success. Some brought us presents. It brought us in mind of our golden wedding....

We are glad that Donald* is getting on so well with his learning. We hope he will come home to finish up his education in Edinburgh...Father joins in love to you all.

Your mother,
Catherine McLaren

*The McLaren's schoolboy son

2   Muirside Farm

The family moved to Muirside Farm when John was about eleven years of age. Sitting in a sheltered hollow at the edge of Bannockburn, Muirside was not so much a farm as a small-holding, a "handkerchief" farm—what in Scotland is called a "croft"—running to some ten or a dozen acres of land.

Bannockburn, in those days, was a quiet place, surrounded by fields and woods and sheltered farms. Traditionally Scottish villages handed down a craft, and one of the crafts handed down in Bannockburn had been weaving. The village, in the mid-nineteenth century, was rustic in character with the homes of the weavers in neat, modest rows. A mill and some sheds stood on the banks of the burn and in these were woven various woolen goods—clothing, blankets, shawls, and the like. During the wars with Napoleon, the mills had supplied the military with some of the articles they needed and this had resulted in a modest prosperity. Later, coal was discovered and pitmen moved in. The pits brought industry and growth—which was good—but the pastoral nature of the village was ultimately lost. In John McLaren's youth, Bannockburn was rural and he grew to manhood among a congenial, gentle people.

Sir Walter Scott used to claim that he could stand on the top of Eildon Hill in Tweeddale and point out forty-three places of historical interest in the Scottish Borders. The same could be said of Muirside Farm. It was surrounded by history. Bannockburn, Stirling, Sheriffmuir, Doune, Cambuskenneth, Sauchieburn, Falkirk! Names famed in Scotland's story and

Muirside Farm, 1899, the year after the scullery was added to the front of the house. Next door is the haybarn with outside ladder.

Scotland's glory—and not one of them more than a day's walk from Muirside Farm. Thirteen battles, it is said, were fought for liberty within the sight of Stirling Castle and Muirside Farm. The whole area was once a battleground as torn and scarred as Homer's "ringing plains of windy Troy" and some of John McLaren's earliest memories were of his father and mother sitting by the Muirside fire (beneath a text from the Bible, "Be strong and of a good courage," hanging on the wall next to the "waggity-wa" clock), telling stories of the Scottish clans—their heroism and pride, their jealousies and petty rivalries, their savage slaughter by the "Butcher," Cumberland, at Culloden. Years later he remembered them. He remembered, too, and never forgot, the ballads his mother taught him as a boy:

> I've heard them liltin' at the ewe-milkin',
> Lasses a-liltin' before dawn o' day;
> But now they are moanin' on ilka green loanin',
> The floors o' the forest are a' wede away."

(The flowers of the forest are all withered away. A reference to the young men slain on Flodden Field in

1513 when the Scots suffered bitter defeat at the hands of the English.)

I have read that when Cromwell was planning his son Richard's education, he said he wanted him to know a little history. John McLaren knew a little of his country's history. All his life he read Scott, whose tales of the Jacobites and Covenanters he revelled in. He particularly like Scott's Rob Roy, the red-haired reiver, with his daring exploits on the braies of Balquhidder, not far from Artalnaig, his mother's girlhood home.

Muirside (where my sister, brothers, and I all were born) was a wonderful place for a child to grow up. A stone's-throw away from the long, low house, across a small pasture, was the "Colonel's Wood." Like Joan of Arc's Forest of Domremy, it was a "magic wonderland." Sycamore, chestnut, beech, and oak all grew there, their roots exposed and tangled like writhing snakes. Mysterious, winding paths ran through it like rabbit-runs. It was in this wood that John McLaren first learned to love trees and appreciate their beauty. He walked through it every day to his work at Bannockburn House, and these daily walks were definitive in his development. Margaret Geddes, his long-time secretary at Golden Gate, used to say that John McLaren could hold an audience spellbound when he spoke about trees—a willow, for example, its roots reaching "over the rocks to find a drink o' water" or a cypress "humping its shoulders tae skook frae the storm." "It was uncanny," she said. "You felt you should bow down before the tree in awesome, mystic reverence." Years later, when he returned on furlough from San Francisco with his wife Jane and his granddaughter Matie (Matie's mother, Martha Leonard, died in childbirth and the McLarens, her paternal grandparents, brought her up), he would hire a two-horse carriage and take trips, usually business trips of a horticultural nature, through the countryside, dining at the best hotels as a special treat for Matie, just a teenager at the time, but, on those furloughs, John McLaren's favorite spot was always the wood. He never failed to go there and walk again the old, remembered boyhood paths. Chateaubriand tells us that he never heard a lark sing but it brought back all his youth. The Colonel's Wood did the same for John McLaren. It brought back memories.

Diagonal to the wood and just a five-minute walk away was the quarry, a different kind of place, sinister and foreboding: the kind of place where hovered Aeschylus' "elemental forces." In the quarry, one always felt that something baleful was about to happen. It was a place which could send icy shivers running up and down the spine. At the foot of a towering escarpment was a hole filled with water, green with slime, and with the stench of death about it. Young John McLaren once saw a suicide there and it left a lasting impression. A poor unfortunate, unable to handle his troubled life, had decided to end it all with a length of rope. The dead man's neck was twice its normal length and his face blue and contorted—a gruesome, grisly spectacle. McLaren, just a boy at the time, couldn't sleep for a week, and as a result was subject to violent nightmares and was on the verge of a nervous breakdown. (During his years at Golden Gate John McLaren kept a file with newspaper cuttings of all who had committed suicide in the park—and there were many, the Golden Gate Bridge not yet having been built—a rather macabre and morbid thing to do. Perhaps the practice had something to do with the emotional wound of his boyhood.)

John McLaren had a normal childhood. When he was fourteen years of age, he saw the laying of the Foundation Stone of the Wallace Monument, a magnificent obelisk, raised to honor William Wallace, Scotland's greatest hero. The Monument stands on the Abbey Craig outside Stirling and can be seen for miles around in any direction. The Stone was laid in 1860 by the Duke of Atholl, Grand Master of Masons in Scotland at the time. Forty bands played "Scots Wha Hae" and a twenty-gun salute was fired from Stirling Castle. The admission fee was expensive—one guinea—and made the occasion rather exclusive, but young John scrambled up the wooded knoll, eluded the man at the gate, and gate-crashed the party. He saw and heard everything for nothing and ever after loved to tell the tale with suitable embellishments.

He also loved to tell of the "Scatter." In Scotland, in the old days, couples were sometimes married in the home, and it was customary for the groom to toss a handful of pennies to the children of the village who always gathered to wave them off as they drove off on their honeymoon. As the coins were thrown, the children scrambled to retrieve what they could of the bounty. This melee was called the "Scatter" and it was, for the children at least, a cut-throat affair with no holds barred. One day, a bridegroom, unusually nervous at the prospect of his married state, got his pockets mixed up. In one, he had half-crowns for the honeymoon and, in the other, pennies for the "Scatter." In his nervousness, he threw out the wrong coins. Young John retrieved half-a-crown in the scrimmage, and immediately hot-footed it to the candy store to buy the place up. How the young honeymooners prevailed without their expenses remains a mystery as the story never got beyond the "wee sweetie shop" and the ensuing over-indulgence.

But it wasn't all fun. The struggle to keep the wolf from the door was always present and the family was never far from the brink of ruin. For a boy the work was heavy—cutting thistles in the meadow before they seeded, pitching hay (a manual task in those days), "mucking" the byre, "thinning" the turnips—and the stocky fourteen-year-old, being the oldest, had to pull his weight.

At the age of fourteen, his schooldays over, he was faced with the problem of earning a living. He had no desire to be a farmer as it was unlikely that he, a poor man's son, would ever be able to buy a place of his own and, therefore, would have to spend the rest of his days working as a farm-laborer, a dismal prospect. But being of independent spirit, he saw no good reason to toil in perpetual bondage to someone else. Also, to work in one of Bannockburn's "dark, satanic mills" would be, for him, a lover of the open air, nothing short of purgatory. He, therefore, decided to become a gardener. To be head gardener on a Scottish estate, working for the gentry, was a job of some standing and gave a measure of freedom and the scope for imaginative creativity. "Gardening is an art," McLaren always said and he rejected, for himself at least, such grand titles as landscape artist, landscape engineer, or arborealist. "Just call me 'Boss Gardener' " he would say with a prideful smile. It was a title he liked.

To John McLaren, gardening was not a career, but a calling. "Career" conjures up a mental image of a runaway horse "careering" down the street, aimless and out of control. "Calling," on the other hand, is a religious word. It has about it a sense of election, discipline, Calvinistic predestination. To John McLaren, in his later life, "growing things" was something to which he felt he had always been "called." It was a profound conviction. He found it hard to believe Sartre's *Rocquentin* that life was "given him for nothing." "Work and life in a garden were the nicest things I could think of as a boy, and I've never changed my mind," he said in his nineties. Years earlier, as a stripling youth, he had made his "pledge with destiny" to spend his life growing things and, having put his hand to the plough, he saw no reason to change—nor did he ever wish to.

3   The Prentice Years

John McLaren's first job was at Bannockburn House, a small estate, encircled by woods, farms, and fields and less than half a mile from his home at Muirside. The owner was Mrs. Wilson, an aristocratic and kindly lady, who attended the same church as the McLarens. She was a widow, and the mother of Colonel Wilson who owned and operated the Bannockburn wool mill. There the fourteen-year-old, half-way to becoming a man, began his long life's work as a master-gardener.

Bannockburn House was handsome. A tree-lined avenue led up to it with the head gardener's house, the "Lodge," at one end, and the stables and the coachman's house at the other. Just before reaching the coach-house, the avenue veered to the right and led to

Bannockburn House.

Prince Charles Edward Stuart (from painting by T. S. Evans).

the Big House, the manor itself. A smaller driveway, set between hedges of laurel, led from the Lodge to the rear of the "Big House" and was for the use of servants and tradesman, for life in Victorian times was not egalitarian.

Bannockburn House was fronted with magnificent, well-kept lawns and at the rear was a large flower and vegetable garden with box-hedge demarcations, rose-covered bowers, and neat graveled paths. A few acres of policies and woodland made up the rest of the property. Prince Charles Edward, the Young Pretender, once stayed there at the time of the Battle of Falkirk, and local tradition has it that it was at Bannockburn House that he first met Clementine Walkinshaw, the mistress who followed him into exile and bore him a daughter, Charlotte, his only child.

Bannockburn House was a good place for a young gardener to start, and the young John McLaren enjoyed his years there, "helping the gardeners," as he put it. There he learned the basics of his calling—how to use a spade, prune a bush, pot a plant, graft a shoot, weave a dream.

Bannockburn House still stands, its stones soaked and beaten with the wind and the sun and the rain, but now just a shadow of its former self, the grounds sadly overgrown and uncared for. A place of frayed gentility. The Wilsons are no more!

After three years with the Wilson family (who did a lot for Bannockburn), McLaren left in March 1864 for Blair Drummond House, five miles northwest of Stirling, a place with richer and more expensive acres. To this early training ground, he also felt deeply indebted. The owner was Mr. Henry Home-Drummond whose daughter Anne married the Duke of Atholl (whom she outlived by thirty-three years), and became a lady-in-waiting to Queen Victoria.

Blair Drummond was renowned for its shrubberies filled with rhododendrons and azaleas, and each spring and summer the gardens were the glory of the district—"like the gardens of Paradise." Here the young boy, seventeen and eager, gained a wider experience and one which was to prove to be of enormous value in future years. It was said of the young Sir Walter that he was "aye makin' himself." John McLaren stayed at Blair Drummond House for three valuable years—working, learning, "makin' himself."

The original Blair Drummond House, the one McLaren knew, was destroyed by fire in 1898. The present turreted, castle-like edifice (now named

Blair Drummond House.

Camphill) was sold some years ago by the then laird,
Sir John Muir. Today it is a school for children
afflicted with cerebral palsy.

In his late teens, John McLaren developed a noble
and intense passion to learn. He was determined to
study, realizing that if ever he was to achieve his
dream of becoming head gardener on a big estate, he
would be required to know more than the practical
side of things. He would also need to know theory.
The spade he felt he knew, but of the microscope, he
had no vestige. He decided, therefore, to apply for a job
at the Royal Botanic Garden, and he also enrolled in
the Botany Class to study Botany (the "gentlest of
sciences") and Taxonomy under Professor Balfour. It
was possible to do this as Scottish education at the
time was such that the poor boy, the "lad o' pairts,"
could work in the spring and summer and earn
enough to pursue a course of study during the winter
months.
      The Royal Botanic Garden was founded in 1670 by
two Edinburgh physicians—Sibbald and Balfour,
(both later knighted), as a "physic garden" to cultivate
and study herbs and plants for healing just as the
hooded monks had done in the Middle Ages. Today it
is a vast teaching establishment of world renown.

McLaren's Edinburgh years were years of great happiness and also years in which he acquired a great deal of horticultural knowledge. He fed upon Balfour's wisdom. He worked and read voraciously and seems to have acquitted himself with some merit as Drs. Harold Fletcher and William Brown write in their *The Royal Botanic Garden, Edinburgh, 1670-1970* of work done, and exhibited by "pupils of the Botany Class." They write of:

> ...framed dissections of flowers, including those of grasses and sedges, of lichens and other non-flowering plants, all executed by former pupils of the Botany Class, including the eminent physician and amateur geologist, Dr. Charles Murchison; another physician and authority on sedges, Dr. (later Sir) W.O. Priestley; Dr. William Lauder Lindsay, the lichenologist and Mr. John McLaren who was to establish the famous Golden Gate Park in San Francisco on a great moving sand dune.

McLaren spent at least one winter and spring in the Botany Class at the Royal Botanic Garden, the intervening springs and summers being spent working in gardens around Edinburgh, at Mavis Bank, or swinging a scythe at the Muirside harvests.

John McLaren did not graduate from the Royal Botanic Garden, if graduation was ever his intention. Fate gave him a nudge and the opportunity to go to America presented itself before he had time to do so— and also, having met a young lady, he wished to get married. To spend several more winters completing a degree course would have taken too long. Whether the lack of a degree was an impediment in later life is debatable. He achieved great success at Golden Gate Park, and won a lasting name without one. ("Can excellence be learned?" asked Socrates.) Perhaps his degreeless state may even have worked to his advantage, for professor Liberty Hyde Bailey, the distinguished horticulturist of Cornell University, once said that he liked the man with an "incomplete course" because such a man is a man with a point of view, not a man with mere facts. "This man," he said, "will see the big and significant things. Later he will consider the details."

John McLaren also worked for a short time at Dupplin Castle, near Perth, seat of the Earl of Kinnoul, with its large plantations of firs covering what once had been a wasteland. The brevity of his stay there suggests that it may have been a summer job taken to earn funds enough for another winter of study in the Botany Class.

One of his last places of employment in Scotland was Gosford, the lordly estate of the Earl of Wemyss, near Haddington in the Lothians. McLaren enjoyed tremendously the various estates on which he worked, for each was a learning experience. But for Bannockburn House, the first, he always had a special affection and for Gosford, the last, he reserved a special corner in his heart. In January 1943, at the time of McLaren's death, a series of interviews given to Mr. J. Lawrence Toole, a San Francisco newspaperman, was published in the *Call-Bulletin* and in one of them McLaren makes reference to the "wonderful gardens" at Gosford. "It might interest you to know," he said to Toole, "that all the gardens and trees there had been grown on what had been sand dunes, just like our gardens and trees in Golden Gate Park."

It was while at the Royal Botanic Garden that John McLaren met Jane Mill, the tall, lovely young Edinburgh girl who would one day be his wife. It was also while in Edinburgh ("too well-known to be described," according to Dr. Johnson) that the golden opportunity came to go to America. Mr. George Howard, heir to a huge bonanza fortune, was scouring Europe looking for an "able gardener with the necessary knowledge and experience" to create a park on his ranch at San Mateo similar to those he had seen in France and Austria. McLaren's name was mentioned, an interview took place, and soon after the young Scot, born with a knack and a touch of genius, set sail for Goethe's "romantic land of freedom" to become head gardener at El Cerrito ("Little Hill"), the Howards' home on the Bay Peninsula. It was there, on six-and-one-half thousand clayey, windswept acres, that the Scottish master gardener's American odyssey began.

4   Rises Your Land of Beyond

> And lo! Far ahead, above the mist and the scud,
> rises your Land of Beyond.
>
> F. Nansen

Mrs. Martha Daniels (McLaren's granddaughter, Matie), wrote in an essay: "In 1872, John McLaren accepted the position of the Howards' Head Gardener to continue the work of building the San Mateo peninsula estate they had named El Cerrito. He left Liverpool by ship a few months later and, after an interrupted voyage of one week in New York, and a trip across Panama by rail, he arrived to take over."

McLaren sailed from Liverpool on December 4, 1872, at the end of the Franco-Prussian War, aboard the *Manhattan*. He travelled tourist-class with a bizarre cast of characters (and an occasional seafaring rat!), dreamers all like himself—domestics, tradesmen, clerks, apprentices, and the like. "A genial and friendly lot," he called them—upbeat, eager, and pleasant to voyage with. "Sailed about 12:50 P.M." says his diary. "Danced in the evening and walked with some very nice ladies." A good enough start!

A young carpenter from Perthshire, an amateur musician, formed a band from those who could play an instrument and there was singing and dancing and music throughout the voyage.

As the ship headed out to the open sea, there was a dramatic change in the weather and the genial and friendly lot, though they did not yet know it, were about to experience one of the worst storms the changeable Atlantic had seen in over twenty years.

The ship that brought McLaren to America.

The *Manhattan* began to roll and pitch like a "drunken drogher" and the waves, mountain high, exploded against her sides and bow like bursting bombs. "Wind right ahead. Nothing but sick people to be seen vomiting in every corner. Got sick myself this afternoon," reads the diary for December 6. The storm seems to have been the "real Atlantic snorter" that the old sailing ship captains used to speak of.

Despite the storm, the seasick mariners made the most of it. They danced, sang, played checkers, chess, and read. There was no radio, but they engaged in "interesting conversations" about Oscar II, the new King of Sweden, and David Livingstone, the missionary/explorer from Blantyre, alone and dangerously ill out in Africa, just weeks away from death. With special interest they discussed Ulysses S. Grant, the president under whose administration their fortunes would henceforth be determined.

The storm howled on, reaching its peak on December 13. "A fearful storm. Can't get on deck. Waves mountains high. No dancing tonight." Sixteen days out from Liverpool was December 20, McLaren's twenty-sixth birthday, and he felt homesick all day. An intense loneliness took hold of him as he thought of Muirside and the family, and Jane, a world away but, when evening came, he wrote a long letter home which helped to rally his spirits and lift his gloom and the family was glad to have his news.

On December 22, they arrived in New York. It was a cold, frosty day. "Sighted land about 1:00 P.M. and anchored about 4:00 P.M. about 40 miles from New York. Land on both sides. Welcome after one of the stormiest passages in 20 years." They steamed up the Hudson in Arctic-like conditions, eager to be ashore. "I have seen Glasgow and Liverpool and a few more of our old-country harbours," he wrote later, "but New York surpasses anything that I have ever seen for size, appearance, or design." Thus did his first sight of America, "Land of the Pilgrims' Pride," impress him, as it has impressed thousands since.

McLaren and his fellow passengers were escorted to Castle Garden in a flat-bottomed boat, Ellis Island, the later launching pad, not yet having been conceived. All around the huge, circular building (a former fort and then an opera house where Jenny Lind, the "Swedish Nightingale," once sang) were signs in different languages for the convenience of the polyglot immigrants. Whatever new arrivals were required to do, was done there. From Castle Garden, the young Scot went to the Swan Hotel on Lower Broadway, where he stayed for a week before continuing his journey west to San Francisco, his future home.

On Christmas day, the Swan was jam-packed with revellers and, to escape the noise, McLaren spent five cents on a trolley ride to Central Park, where he walked for a time—but not for long, as the temperature was sub-zero. Writing later to Jane, he told of how he had seen in the Park a statue of "Tam-o-Shanter and Souter Johnny takin' their dram fu' canty." (To John McLaren, as to many Scots still, Robert Burns was an object of worship and someone to be quoted endlessly! And why not? He is a poet worth quoting.)

On December 26 he visited three places—the Waterfront, where he saw ships of many lands, the

Museum of Natural History, and the New York Zoo—
all of which impressed him.

One evening an incident took place which induced
him to change his plans. A group of young Welsh
miners arrived at the Swan. They were returning
from the Comstock Lode in Virginia City, Nevada,
where the work had slackened off. Because of this
they had decided to return to their lonely Welsh
mountains. The lad from the farmlands of Stirling
spoke with them and they persuaded him to change
his itinerary. It had been McLaren's intention to go
west by train in order to see something of the size,
color, and variety of the land to which he had come.
But the returning men of Harlech, having made the
overland journey, advised against it on the grounds
that it was long, tedious, and risky. Landslides and
cave-ins were common, the Indians (the "Men of
Always") sometimes grew restive and broke out of
their reservations to attack locomotives and wreak
general havoc. And there were desperadoes like Frank
and Jesse James and Cole Younger and his brothers,
who had graduated from robbing banks to robbing
trains. The upshot was that McLaren decided to travel
by sea to Panama, cross the isthmus by train (the
Canal not yet having been built), and then continue up
the West Coast by ship to San Francisco.

How wise this decision was is debatable. Panama
was no Garden of Eden. Cholera was rife, as was
yellow fever and dysentery, and it no doubt had
desperadoes of its own, but McLaren seems not to have
weighed the consequence. He travelled via Panama
and ultimately arrived in San Francisco healthy and
none the worse for wear. Indeed, crossing the isthmus
proved to be the highlight of his journey.

On the last day of 1872, the staunch, dyed-in-the-
wool Presbyterian attended Evensong in Trinity
Church at the head of Wall Street ("allowed to be one of
the finest in the city"), probably because there was no
Presbyterian church nearby. He adjudged the choir to
be "very fine" but makes no assessment of the
sermon—if there was one.

At the stroke of midnight on December 31, New

Year's Eve, all at the Swan joined brotherly and sisterly hands and sang a verse of "Auld Lang Syne" which, no doubt, "garred the saut tear blin' his ee" as he thought of the folks back home in Scotland. Next day, January 1, 1873, McLaren left New York for San Francisco and journey's end, a journey that was to take him almost one month.

5   New Scenes, New Faces

McLaren sailed from New York on the *Ocean Queen,* a twenty-seven hundred tonner, part of the Pacific Mail Steamship Company's flotilla. She was sturdy and well-built with "the thrill of life along her keel" (to quote the poet), but "she could have done with a good lick of paint to make her look better," observed the young Scot somewhat less poetically. Her appearance notwithstanding, the *Ocean Queen* was adequate and McLaren felt fortunate to have secured a berth.

She weighed anchor on January 1, 1873, New Year's Day. The temperature was twenty below zero, the coldest weather the Scottish farm boy had ever experienced and, although he had enjoyed his stay in New York, he was looking forward to escaping to the sun.

The sail round the coast was pleasant. In no time they were in the sapphire waters of the Gulf. By day the sun shone endlessly, and at night McLaren would stand on the deck looking up at the sky, speckled with stars, existentially contemplating the music of the spheres, the dark sea, and Thales' "mother of life," while the craft rose and fell with a gentle motion, her rigging creaking softly.

The first stop was Havana, a hundred miles south of the Florida Keys. The young gardener enjoyed watching the longshoremen at work, their skin glistening with sweat, and thought the mood of the Cuban people a happy one despite the fact that de Cespedos' revolution was in progress at the time. Next came Aspinwall in Panama, named for the New York

McLaren departed New York City on the Ocean Queen, *bound for California.*

shipping merchant who had built a railroad across the isthmus a few years earlier in the 1850s, thus providing the short-cut which had proved such a boom in the Gold Rush years. The Canal had not yet been built, and it was by Aspinwall's railroad that commuters were shunted back and forth from the Atlantic to the Pacific.

This phase of his journey, and the later sail up the California coast, McLaren enjoyed tremendously. In the Toole interviews he says:

> That trip was one of the nicest experiences of my life up to then. New scenes, new places, new people and new trees and plants and flowers. It cost me to look around. That was two shillings in Scotch money, quite a bit to a lad as poor as I was then, but it was worth it; aye, every penny of it. I found trees and plants and flowers I'd heard and read about. I saw my first coconut tree at Punta Arenas and I remember my interest swithering between that and the wee, brownish bairns hanging in hammocks on the walls outside the houses, jist like flowers.

As the train dawdled its way across the isthmus and he looked out across the landscape, the young gardener was impressed by the tropical trees—palms, papayas, carbanjos, etc.—growing wild and in profusion. "I saw among other things," (he wrote to Jane in February, a few weeks later), "the date coconut, the Orange Eucharis, the Ficus Elastica, the Ficus Camea and the Caladium Dickinson." These he had studied under glass in Edinburgh, and now recognized growing in the wild.

He travelled up the coast on yet another ship, the mailboat *Montana,* a screw steamer, built (I believe) in Maine. On this last leg of his journey several shore visits were made, and at no time were they ever very far from land. In a letter he wrote to Jane on February 25, 1873 he says:

> We called at seven places along the coast which retarded our progress very much. At some, we spent one or two days but it was very pleasant. The sun shone every day. Every place we called at, the Indians and Mexicans came swarming aboard the ship, shouting like Newhaven fishwives, only they were in canoes as the vessel could not get in, the water not being deep enough. The first place we called at when it was dark and they had torches in their hands. It was a queer sight to see the reds swarming all around, crying 'oranges, cigars, parrots, etc.' It reminded me of Burn's scene at Alloway Kirk, described so well in his tale of Tam-o-Shanter.

On one of those shore visits McLaren had a moment of "confrontation," as the Barthians used to say. He had entered into an agreement with a native to be ferried ashore and back for a certain sum. On the way back the boatman reneged, and demanded double. McLaren pointed out as best he could that such was not the arrangement. The native, who spoke only Spanish, became eloquently abusive and refused to ferry him back, whereupon McLaren, small in stature, but husky and strong, his adrenaline pumping, scooped him up like a babe in arms and threatened to throw him into the ocean. The boatman capitulated and the original contract was honored.

At Punta Arenas in Costa Rica, (a place which had not seen rain for four years), McLaren met an old Scotsman, the only white man in the place. He had lived there for twenty-five years and had taken an Indian squaw, a woman half his age, with black eyes and still blacker hair pulled back in the classic manner. They had a "few half-red bairns" and the man appeared to have grown quite prosperous among his Indian friends. The two traded sentimental gossip about Scotland for a while, and the old-timer seemed to enjoy the civilized chat, but I do not think my great-uncle, a fairly good judge of character, was overly impressed with him. He seemed to be a man without scruple. A "bit of a bounder."

Life aboard the *Montana* was pleasant. There was singing and dancing each night—Steele's "Nights of mirth and jollity"—the music being provided by three fiddles, two flutes, a concertina and, of all things, a set of Scottish bagpipes! This collection of raggle-taggle musicians was willing to play as long as there was anyone who wished to dance, sing, or just listen.

After stops at Acapulco, Manzanillo, Mazatlan, Cape San Lucas, and San Diego (just a small town then), the *Montana* steamed north for San Francisco, arriving on the morning of January 30, 1973. The

On January 30, 1873 the Montana *arrived in San Francisco, carrying a passenger who was to make a lasting impression on the city.*

weather was mild and warm. As the ship rounded
Fort Point and nosed gently into the Bay, the Scottish
crofter's son was struck by the beauty of the city, the
"houses piled on top of one another, hugging the sides
of the hills." They were built of wood, as were the
sidewalks. When he first saw Market Street, McLaren
was reminded of Edinburgh and knew he was "here
to stay." That night, January 30, he put up at the New
Wisconsin Hotel. The following day was spent sight-
seeing and, in the evening, he went to the California
Theatre to see Mr. John McCullough, a noted actor, in
performance of "Rob Roy," which no doubt brought
back memories of home.

McLaren was glad to be in San Francisco, the city
to which he was later to become so profoundly
attached, as he was "heartily sick of the sea." After
five days of seeing the sights and visiting people from
the old country, he went on to El Cerrito, the Howard
estate, fifteen miles away in San Mateo where, in
early February 1873 at the age of twenty-six, he
assumed his duties as head gardener.

The *Alta Californian,* in its January 31 issue of
1873, makes an interesting comment on McLaren and
his fellow-passengers aboard the *Montana.* Its
columns that day carried the following report:

Arrival Of Scotch Immigrants

The steamship *Montana* which arrived in
port yesterday brought 48 Scotch
immigrants who came out here to fill
positions of servants and laborers. Some
months ago, several parties resident in this
city, requiring the services of good,
trustworthy servants, sent an agent to
Scotland who finally succeeded in
obtaining the above number. The passage
money for the whole trip was to be
deducted from their wages. They left
Glasgow, December 12th, remaining in

New York for a few days prior to coming here. There are 18 females among the number who are engaged as servants in families in this city. The whole party appear to be a bright, intelligent class of people, differing greatly from the average class of immigrant which usually arrives here.

6　El Cerrito

There were quite a number of Scottish gardeners in San Francisco at the turn of the century, transplants all, who had quit their native shores to seek a new heaven and a new earth on California's golden soil. Most of them seemed to prosper, but none left the mark that John McLaren, the boy from Bannockburn did.

Even before the completion of the transcontinental railroad in the 1850s and 1860s, the San Mateo Peninsula became home to a number of wealthy landowners—the Ralstons, Stanfords, Floods, Ogden Millses and so on—who built sumptuous private estates on the land they bought from Spanish ranchers. One of those "Nobs" was Mr. George Howard, heir to a vast mining fortune made a generation earlier. His family had acquired Rancho San Mateo, six-and-one-half acres, which they re-named "El Cerrito." It had originally been bought by W. D. M. Howard, his brother. Later, Mr. George Howard and Agnes, his beautiful and charmingly coquettish wife, took it over and when George Howard died, Agnes then married Henry Pike Bowie who became the new chatelaine of the rancho. It was the George Howards who engaged McLaren in Edinburgh and he worked for them at El Cerrito and, later, for the Bowies after George Howard's death and Mrs. Agnes Howard's remarriage.

El Cerrito, one of the largest of the peninsula estates, "set the pace of fashion for two generations on the peninsula." Today, it is no more. The site is covered by freeways, houses, supermarkets, and gas stations. Little remains of the open land, the pastures, the farm, the dairy, the orchards, the lawns and paths, the hedges, fountains, and rosegardens with which McLaren surrounded the house, a rather ostentatious, Victorian structure which had been prefabricated in Boston, transported by ship around the Horn, and set in place just west of the highway El Camino Real.

McLaren's mission at El Cerrito was to transmute a wasteland into a Garden of Eden, a staggering assignment, but McLaren was always at his best when working on the heroic scale and when confronted with a challenge. A flower garden was already in existence. This McLaren had to maintain, but his specific task at the rancho was to "create a landscape similar to those seen in Europe." To do so involved the planting of endless trees, the building of roads and bridges, the redirecting of streams, the laying of miles of pipeline, and the construction of flumes and waterfalls. It was a mammoth task, multifaceted in range, but McLaren was confident and determined to conquer.

He began by hiring teams of horses and men, mostly Irish and Chinese, two ethnic groups, poor and hunger-driven, who did not always get along, but McLaren had little trouble with them. He possessed a remarkable facility for handling men. Later, in 1894, W.W. Stow, President of the Board of Commissioners at Golden Gate Park, wrote to General R. P. Hammond: "He [McLaren] is a rare man, and if anyone doubts his being a Major-General, let him go out yonder and see him handle two thousand men."

The success he enjoyed at El Cerrito, McLaren owed to zeal, amazing know-how and savvy, and prodigious hard work. As with Cecil Rhodes, his "enterprises were his passions." He revelled in challenge and responsibility and was an incomparable work-a-holic. Throughout life, it was his practice to rise at dawn ("That's when I get my best licks in!") and continue untiringly at the job until the sun went down. His men were expected to do the same, and if a job was going slowly, McLaren would sometimes grab a spade from a man's hand (according to Mr.

The Howard Homestead

Frank Foehr, a later superintendent), all the while inveighing against him for his lack of expertise in its use. The man, of course, would be wielding the tool quite properly, but McLaren's action would make him seethe with inner rage, and mumbling threats of murder beneath his breath, he would return to his digging with increased vigor. "An angry man always works harder" was McLaren's stated philosophy.

John McLaren remained at El Cerrito for fourteen years, from 1873-1887. While his chief employers were the owners of El Cerrito, he also did landscaping work for several other "Nobs" in the area—Leland Stanford, the railroad magnate who became Governor of the State and also founded Stanford University; James Lick, who bequeathed sixty thousand dollars for a monument to Francis Scott Key of "The Star-Spangled Banner"; W.C. Ralston, the "builder of San

Donnelly—Burlingame.

Francisco," who drove into, and out of, the city each day, with his spanking team from his estate, Belmont, changing horses on the way; and John Donnelly, who is said to have built the first home in Burlingame. And there were others too—the Poetts, Maglees, Hoyts, and Ogden Millses. These all were a little colony of the rich, an "oligarchy of plutocratic wealth," in the San Mateo and Millbrae areas. Most of them had homes in San Francisco, but also so-called "summer cottages" in San Mateo and other places.

In San Mateo, McLaren planted thousands and thousands of trees. In one year, he planted nine avenues with 2,250 elms, 3,250 pines, 20,000 gums, and 300 red gums. The *Redwood City Tribune,* writing at the time, stated that McLaren "planted on Bellevue, Poplar Avenue, Monte Diablo Avenue, Tilton Avenue and St. John's Cemetery, all in San Mateo." He also planted 70,000 trees (one thousand per acre) on the seventy-acre Coyote Point at the Howards, which the Irish and Chinese laborers performed "in record time."

One of his projects while on the Peninsula was to plant El Camino Real from San Mateo Creek to Millbrae. The concept was born one evening at a meeting held in the George Howard dining room. Present were such Olympians as Alfred Poett, D. Ogden Mills, Arthur Reddington, and W.C. Ralston. Howard, the project's moving spirit, presided, and John McLaren attended as head gardener and technical advisor. It should be pointed out that these grandees were not simply being advocates of arboreal taste out to beautify the highway. They were also hard-headed businessmen out to enhance their holdings in the event of future sales. They weren't millionaires for nothing!

The execution of the project was left to John McLaren, each of the participants being financially responsible for the planting of his own frontage. Thousands of elms and eucalyptuses would act as "nurse trees," setting up a windbreak to protect the young elms until they rooted. Later, the eucalyptuses would be removed. The original plan, however, was not implemented. The eucalyptuses were not removed as George Howard died and John McLaren later left for Golden Gate Park. Years afterwards (when at Golden Gate), McLaren observed that "the eucalyptuses had been permitted to overshadow and ruin the elms." The giant eucalyptuses, over a hundred years old, still stand, tall and stately sentinels, buffeted by the winds,

Ralston—Belmont.

along the magnificent highway. My wife and I drove along it, in all its royal splendor, on Palm Sunday, 1987, and saw the very trees my great-uncle had planted a century before. A magnificent and awesome spectacle.

The Howard and Bowie families travelled frequently in Europe, sometimes for prolonged periods, and McLaren was required to submit written reports (of which he always kept careful copies) of the work being done. A letter written to the young George Howard, grandson of the gold-mining pioneer, in 1880 reads:

Dear Mr. George,

I am glad you are coming home soon. If you were here now you would like it very much, I am sure. The place looks the brightest green, the oaks just leafing out and the light tea green of the white oak harmonizing so well with the darker oaks and bays. I was at Menlo Park last Sunday but there is no place to compare with El Cerrito. Stanford and Flood are spending

Stanford Barn

fortunes in buying the newest varieties of plants and trees from all over the world but they cannot give their places the free and natural appearance of this place in spring. I have seen Maggie* twice. She seems very lonesome since she left you all. I don't know if she is doing anything or not. The trip seems to have done her good. I hope you have all benefitted from your trip. Remember us to Mr. and Mrs. Bowie, Miss Julie Howard, Miss Babette and Master Harry.

> Yours Respectfully,
> John McLaren

*Probably a lady's maid. (Maggie Miller who became the McLarens' housekeeper at Golden Gate?)

In the above, McLaren writes of the "free and natural appearance" he had achieved in El Cerrito. Like Wordsworth, he believed in a "return to Nature." He always strove for the "natural look, eschewing artificiality. Nature seldom runs in straight lines," he often said, or "Why must people change beautiful things?" He was an invincible Romanticist. He possessed great aesthetic perception and the Romanticist approach achieved at El Cerrito seems to have won local acclaim as a newspaper in 1881 referred to the gardens there as "among the handsomest in the State." Already he was making a name for himself.

McLaren's reports to his employers were sometimes short and pithy, like that of March 23, 1881: "Since you left, have raised 80,000 gum trees, did important rock-work, planted lower side of new walk with violets, have hand-planted 30,000 poplars, 250 maples, 500 cypress." Sometimes they were long and detailed, giving not only an account of what had been done, but also a vision of things hoped for, with some political gossip thrown in for good measure. The following is a report sent to Mr. Bowie in 1880:

Dear Sir,

I was very glad to hear from you and that you are all well. I hope that Miss Babette continues to improve. Yes, I am looking forward to having the seeds from the Jardin des Plantes and expect some rare varieties, also to seeing the plan of the garden at the Palace of Versailles. I am glad our waterfall compares so favourably with those famous ones you have seen. I don't believe there can be any artificial falls or fountains to beat it. If you find any on your travels let me know, also if you see something to add to or improve this one. I am interested in the undergrowth you described so well. Could you send me a few of the names beside acacia? I would like to plant all the bare places on the mound and near the house just as you described it. The nuts are not included in the orchard sale. We gathered 11 sacks of almonds but while we were busy picking plums the boys stole many of the walnuts. We caught five and had them put in jail.

I wrote to Philadelphia about the purple beech. We can get them 23 feet high for 40 dollars a hundred. I ordered 50 which should make a nice group. We have raked all the roads and cleaned up generally. Also transplanted 8,000 gums (after spending a week at the dam). In my next letter, I will give you an account of the varieties of trees we planted on the hills and in the Coyote Canyon which are growing very fast now. The place is much improved.

I emptied the pond and cleaned it out and spread a layer of asphalt over the cracks so that now it is quite dry, not the least sign of moisture in the drain. We took the gums from the shade house to the vegetable garden to harden them but I will cover them on frosty nights.

Politics are running high now. Jasynsky is running against six others for justice and there are nine for Constable. Burns has the Republican nomination for Senator and Mr. Felton of Menlo Park for Assemblyman. I don't remember anything else worth mentioning.

Yours Respectfully,
John McLaren

While at El Cerrito, McLaren created an inconceivably beautiful violet garden for Mrs. Bowie, and while abroad on her vacations she would sometimes become "homesick for her violets." The story has a touching sequel. Mrs. Bowie, for whom McLaren had a very real and warm affection (some say it was she who had hired him in Edinburgh), died in 1893. When he was invited, years later, to plan and supervise the Panama-Pacific International Exposition held in San Francisco in 1915, the bare, drab walls of the building offended his artistic eye and, therefore, on February 25, "San Mateo Day," he had the walls covered with masses of violets, "literally a ton of violets with the dew still on them." Every visitor that day was given a small bunch as a memento. The action was hailed as a piece of horticultural genius—"the only new idea in landscaping since the heyday of ancient Rome," one critic put it, rather fulsomely. It was seen as a piece of horticultural wizardry, but it was also a magnificent "beau gest" made to the memory of Mrs. Bowie, and Mr. Henry Bowie, who was present at the Exposition, was deeply moved. When complimented on his feat, McLaren replied with typical verbal husbandry, "It was a simple thing."

After three years at El Cerrito, McLaren invited Jane to join him. She sailed from Glasgow to New York, crossed the country by train, and stayed with friends in San Francisco until the day of her wedding. She and John McLaren were married on July 31, 1876, reportedly in the Russ House which was destroyed by

Jane Mill McLaren

fire during the earthquake of 1906. No honeymoon followed the nuptials, so pressing was the work at El Cerrito.

Jane Mill McLaren was in many ways a clone of his own mother, Catherine. She was tall and dignified and rather handsome, sternly competent, and a strict disciplinarian. She was the daughter of an extremely Victorian father. Like Catherine Walker McDougall, she could be forbidding at times, but she was also gentle, patient, and kind. She did generous things. And when serving afternoon tea each day at the Lodge, (which was a Means of Grace to her) she was a hostess most gracious. She always dressed in purple, was respected by all, and was an excellent correspondent, maintaining a faithful contact over the years with her sister-in-law, my grandmother, who loved her dearly. In later life, she was lame as the result of a fall on a polished American Oak floor, and carried a gold-headed cane to support herself. She would lean on her cane, her proud chin pointing in the direction she wished to go.

The McLaren's only child, a son, was born in 1879 in San Mateo and named Donald after his paternal grandfather, the Scottish shepherd. Donald died in 1925, preceding both his parents who, from that time on, knew "the fellowship of those who bear the Mark of Pain." Donald's death was their life's great sorrow. "But that," as Kipling used to say, "is another story."

During his years in San Mateo, McLaren worked hard, achieved much, and won the respect and recognition of his peers. He also led a busy social life, joining the Ancient Order of United Workmen, the Lawn Bowling Club, the Oddfellows, and the Masonic Order. He cut a large swath for himself and when he left the township to assume his duties at Golden Gate Park, the *Redwood City Times and Gazette* ran a complimentary piece which ended: "Mr. McLaren is a man of many friends and though we are very sorry to lose him, we are glad that he is to have a larger field for his undoubted talents."

7 Golden Gate Park

It was in Golden Gate Park that John McLaren made his name. In the 1860s San Francisco, pulsing with life, was an interesting and adventurous city, starting to emerge from its wild, pioneering, gold-strike days and reaching out towards an urbane respectability. Frederick Law Olmsted, the nation's most renowned town-planner (and the man who gave us the term "green belt"), was going the rounds preaching that "a park gives a city a soul." The San Francisco City Fathers felt it was time their city had a "soul" and, consequently, they bought 1013 acres of windswept wasteland, part of the "Outside Lands," for $800,000, a price that the citizenry of the time thought a woeful waste of money. Indeed, the purchase was regarded with a certain amount of amusement and referred to as a "white elephant," "not worth a button," and "a joke." Public attention at the time, and the attention of the Park Commissioners, was focused on the building of a race-track which had the support of influential citizens—William Kent, C.P. Huntington, Leland Stanford, W.W. Stow, et al—and the *San Francisco Chronicle* took up the cause:

> Since the early days of wild mining speculation the financial condition of San Francisco has steadily improved until now we have thousands of men whose fortunes, large and small are based on sound investments. Among the wealthier of these capitalists the feeling has been growing stronger year by year that a

healthy interest in horses be fostered here as it is in every city of the eastern states...Now fewer good horses are driven or ridden in San Francisco than any other city of its size in English-speaking countries. Over and over the men who can afford such horses claim that they must have a place for fast-driving and their wish is soon to be granted in Golden Gate Park.

The track was built in 1890, but John McLaren's name is nowhere mentioned in connection with the project. One can only assume that his mind was centered on other matters, such as the reclamation of the sand dunes to the west of Strawberry Hill, and it soon became clear that he was no ordinary gardener. In the early 1890s the public became acutely aware that it was he who was deciding the direction in which the Park should go.

The purchase of the "Outside Lands" had not been easy. There was a long legal battle with "squatters" who knew only too well the old Spanish pueblo laws regarding boundaries and they held out for all they could get. It is a long, involved story, but the upshot is that the purchased land eventually became Golden Gate Park, today a "must-see" for the tourist, and the city's greatest glory.

William Hammond Hall, a Maryland-born engineer, was appointed first Superintendent, a position he held from 1871-1876. He carried out a survey, built some roads, partially developed the Panhandle area, sowed grass, and planted some trees. He also started a playground for children and credit must always be given to him for the work he did though it must also be remembered that Hall was an engineer and not a gardener. McLaren had infinitely more imagination, vision, and horticultural know-how. Hall resigned because of "skulduggery" among officials (and the fact that he was a Southerner did not serve to make him overly popular either).

Three Superintendents followed Hall in quick succession—William Bond Prichard (also a

Southerner; an army officer who had surrendered with Lee at Appomattox); F.P. Hennessey (a rather quick-tempered Irishman who lasted for a year); and John J. McEwen (a teamster from Canada who lasted for four). All were good enough men, in no way guilty of mismanagement, but found it hard, it seems, to work with the "power elite" set over them and so either resigned or were summarily dismissed. The ten years following William Hammond Hall's administration were poor years for Golden Gate Park.

In 1887, John McLaren was appointed Assistant Superintendent. He came well recommended. The Howard family supported him in a letter, a balance sheet of his experience, to the Board of Park Commissioners:

Dear Sirs,

Mr. John McLaren has been employed as head gardener at El Cerrito for the past fifteen years, during which time he has had the direction and management of all matters pertaining to the Arboricultural and Horticultural interests of the property. I consider him a thorough and competent Florist, Landscape Gardener and Forester, well-read and instructed in all branches of his proffesion [sic]. His character for sobriety, honesty and devotion to the interests instructed to him leave nothing to be desired and it is with every confidence that I recommend him to your favourable consideration.

I remain,
Dear Sirs,
W.H. Howard

The Howards also wrote to Major R.P. Hammond, a member of the Board, in more personal terms, praising McLaren as a "first class gardener in all its branches who has made a thorough study of our native trees, shrubs and flora and understands the climate" and who brought about a "great improvement" in San Mateo.

Forty-one-year-old McLaren was given the post, and three years later was appointed full Superintendent of Parks (of which there were several), a position he held for almost fifty-six years, until he died on January 12, 1943, in his 97th year. They were years in which he made his predestinating contribution and showed himself to be no ordinary master gardener. When he started in Golden Gate Park

John McLaren, about age sixty.

there were forty gardeners working under him. When he died that number had increased to almost four hundred, sometimes more at certain seasons of the year for some work was seasonal and, at such times, men would move in from Utah and other places.

His most dramatic work was carried out in the early years, in the 1890s, before the earthquake which reduced much of the city to rubble. These were the spectacular years when Nature was brought under control. Nevertheless, he never rested on his laurels. He continued to construct other city parks and squares, develop the golf links of Lincoln and Harding Parks, the course at Sharp Park at the edge of the ocean near the San Mateo County line, and design the gardens for the 1915 Exposition, planting them with trees and shrubs raised in Park nurseries for the purpose. He worked from dawn till dusk each day until the day he died, but his greatest monument is Golden Gate Park which, in the early years, expressed the rhapsodic spirit of highland verse with its mountain streams plunging down steep cliffs and its tall pines battling with the adverse winds of heaven.

To give a detailed analysis of the work of more than half a century in an essay such as this would be impossible. It would also be redundant as an enormous amount has been written, and in many places, of McLaren's Golden Gate career.* A few highlights, however, are in order.

First, Superintendent John McLaren tamed the unleashed power of the wind and the sea. He himself writes of the havoc wrought by those two forces:

> The sand dunes of San Francisco, are situated in the extreme westerly portion of

---

The Making of Golden Gate Park; The Early Years and *The Making of Golden Gate Park; The Growing Years,* both by Raymond H. Clary, a reliable historian.

the city and, bordering on the Pacific Ocean, lie entirely open and exposed to the storms of winter and to the summer winds which blow nearly every afternoon during the latter season at the rate of twenty or more miles per hour....On account of the almost constant action of the wind, the sand was formerly kept ever on the move, and in heavy gales, drifted like snow, at times being moved in a single day to a depth of three or four feet and often being carried a distance of over a hundred feet.

McLaren sought to "persuade the sea-wave not to break" (to quote Aeschylus), a troubling puzzle. He did so by anchoring, with posts in the sand, thousands of bales of laths and spreading branches and tree-clippings round them. When the tides receded more, sand covered the bales. More bales, with tree-trimmings, were set on top of the first layer. Year after year the process was repeated until, finally, a barrier was created, giving protection from the unrelenting onslaught of the sand and sea. "If you can't work against the sea," said McLaren, "you must use it to work in your favor." He always sought to work with Nature, never against her. The result of his patient use of the tides and the wind gave not only a protective barricade to the Park, but also a magnificent esplanade to the city. He saved the beach by controlling, in Newbolt's phrase, the "eternal, wandering sea."

Second, McLaren conquered the problem of the moving sand. When he first arrived at Golden Gate only the Panhandle, away from the ocean, had been partially developed. West of the Panhandle was nothing but sand. McLaren succeeded in "tying down" the sand. Barley seed had first been tried. A quick sprouter, it held the sand for a time but, being a shallow rooter, it died in a month or two, and therefore, the experiment with barley was abandoned. Next came Yellow Lupine, a strong-growing, perennial shrub. This worked, but only in certain areas where there was some protection. It was not a universal panacea. Success came with sea-bent grass. McLaren was not the first to use it in the Park, but he used it widely, being well aware of its success in Europe and in Scotland. He had loads of seeds imported from Europe. These were sown in the nursery and two years later the tender, young plants were set out and their deep roots held the sand. No matter how deeply the sea-bent was covered by the sand, their crowns would push up to the surface and thus the drift was halted. Layers of topsoil were then spread, Kentucky blue grass sown, and cypresses, madronas, manzanitas, laurels, and other native trees planted. The reclamation did not happen quickly. Like the building of Rome, it took more than a day, but McLaren had the patience to wait and the possibility of failure never even occurred to him. "If he planted ten trees that didn't grow," said one of his foremen, "he'd plant an eleventh that did." McLaren was persistent and stubborn.

He also knew his business. During his years in San Mateo, he had made a study of the climate and conditions prevailing on the California coast, and had carried out experiments so that when he came to Golden Gate he had some idea of what would work and what would fail. This knowledge he later incorporated in a book whose first edition was so soon exhausted that a second, and then a third, had to be produced in order to satisfy public demand. He was clearly a man who knew his job and whose expertise was much respected.

One of the Boss Gardener's great contributions was his creation of the Park's artificial lakes. (His greatest contribution of course was keeping politics out of the Park! "What do politicians know about gardening?" he would snort!) When he first suggested the creation of lakes, he was laughed to scorn. "Behold this dreamer! The water will seep through the sand," the sceptics scoffed. Prophets of doom notwithstanding, the stubborn Scot persisted with his seemingly hopeless and ridiculously ambitious plan. Hundreds of workmen levelled off the ground and excavated the hole for the lake. Load after load of clay was then carted in to cover the sides and bottom. This was "puddled" so that there would be no seams. When this first layer was hard and dry, a second was superimposed, "puddling" again taking place. The area was then filled with fresh water drawn, with windmills, from a well. The first lake was Stow, created in 1892, and named for W. W. Stow, President of the Board of Park Commissioners at the time. Wrote McLaren:

> His great hobby was of course Stow Lake, for which he gave $60,000 in 1892. It was also through his effort that we got Huntington Falls. I told him that a water fall built on that hill would be an attraction. "How much would it cost?" he asked and, when I told him he said, "I'll hunt somebody up who will pay for it. He had Mr. Huntington out there in two days and we soon had the money.

Some would say that Huntington Falls, with its great dramatic power, was McLaren's greatest achievement. Walking one day in the Sierras with John Muir, the Naturalist, his friend, and fellow-Scot from Dunbar, Muir showed him a waterfall he had discovered in a gorge. "You've nothing like that in your Park, John," twitted Muir. "No," replied the grey-eyed dreamer, "but we will have." The Boss Gardener felt that if San Franciscans couldn't get out to the Sierras to see the fall, he could take the waterfall to them. He discussed the possibility with Stow, the Board President, estimating that the project would cost about $25,000. The following Sunday, Stow took McLaren and Collis P. Huntington, the railroad baron, for a buggy ride in the Park. When they reached Strawberry Hill (an eminence where wild strawberries once grew), Stow, addressing Huntington said, "Mac says we could have a fine falls here, running down Strawberry Hill into Stow Lake." "Oh," said Huntington with seeming detachment. But the seed had been sown. A few days later, Huntington's bond was received. (Stow and McLaren were a remarkable team. It was under Stow's regime that so much was accomplished, including the water system, the windmills, the aviary, etc. McLaren also seemed to work well with A.B. Spreckels, another commissioner).

Huntington Falls was opened in 1894. Raymond Clary describes it as being a "fall of 125 feet, the water varying from 3 to 12 feet in width. First, the water rolled lazily down a fall of 6 feet; then it ran down a picturesque cascade of 150 feet and under a rustic bridge to the main fall—a drop of 25 feet, 12 feet in width. Artificial rocks formed the sides of the falls, and the hillside was ornamented with deciduous shade trees, including elm, maple, beech, linden, and birch. Under these trees, more than ten thousand ferns had been planted, mostly natives."

Stow Lake was followed by others—Spreckels (seven acres in extent and a playground for yachtsmen through the years); Lloyd Lake; Metson (McLaren's favorite); Quarry Lake (created from a hole left after quarrying rock to build roads); Alvord Lake; Middle Lake; the Chain of Lakes, and others.

About the Chain of Lakes, McLaren wrote:

> When the foliage becomes more abundant and the grass begins to grow, this will be the prettiest section of the park. It has been our object all along to avoid anything which would tend to destroy the illusion of nature. No harsh palms or stiff groupings will be permitted around the lakes and everything will be done to enhance the natural beauty of the surroundings. On the western slopes we have planted a number of deciduous trees as an experiment. They comprise the eastern sweet gum, maple, ash, tulip and swamp cypress. Under these trees, great masses of rhododendrons will be planted.

When they were working on the Chain of Lakes, the noise of the men and horse scrapers disturbed hummingbirds nesting in a nearby bush. McLaren ordered his men not to frighten them and "Do you ken," he said, "those two wee birds got to know us and to have no fear and when the wee ones came hopping and flying around, and squeaking, they didn't show fear either."

John McLaren was proud of the lakes he created, little highland lochans, with their wooded islands, coves, and marshy spots where wild birds still nest. It is disturbing, therefore, to read in Raymond Clary's history: "The Chain of Lakes today is a scene of desolation and neglect—the product of uncaring commissioners and a penny-wise, pound-foolish city administration." Organization conspicuous by its absence.

McLaren spent more than half a century creating grace and beauty, Ruskin's "vein of wealth," in Golden Gate Park, the place he called his "garden." He built roads, bridges, lakes, and planted thousands and thousands of trees from every country. In his book, he writes:

> On this one thousand acre tract which originally was a waste of drifting, barren sand, may now be found groves of handsome trees, natives of many countries of both hemispheres and of all continents. Here, one may see the Cedar of Lebanon and of Mount Atlas, as well as the Deodar of the Himalayas, the Araucaria of Chile, Brazil and Norfolk Island, also the large-flowering, handsomely foliaged Magnolia of our Southern States, the Elm of New England, and the Sequoia, Cypress, Pine, etc. of our own State. In addition may be found the yew of Old England and the fragrant, feathery Acacia of Australia, together with groves of Bamboos, masses of gaily-flowered Camellias and Rhododendrons and stately Rubber trees,

while hundreds of other varieties of trees and shrubs are to be seen, natives of many climes, all of them apparently happy and healthy in their new surroundings.

He created rose gardens of great beauty, wooded ridges, rhododendron dells, meandering lanes, grassy lawns, meadows for sheep and peacocks (sacred to Juno), and paddocks for buffalo and swift-running deer. There is the world-famous Japanese Garden where kimono-clad maids still serve jasmine tea, and centers for culture like the Museum and the Music Conservatory. There are tennis courts and ball parks where generations of the young first learned to hold a racquet or swing a bat. Some of them turned out to be stars—tennis legends like Helen Jacob and Helen Wills Moody, and baseball "greats," like "Joltin' Joe" DiMaggio, the homerun slugger. Through the years, the Park has given inspiration to artists, writers, and poets. "George Stirling used to walk around here and so did Jack London. I got to know them well," McLaren often said. "McLaren met virtually every important personage who visited San Francisco," wrote Lawrence Toole. "Royalty of every land, presidents, senators, millionaires, merchants of immense renown, famous writers, artists, poets and philosophers, world-known pundits in every art and science and most of the botanists, horticulturists and gardeners in the history of his own art."

It is given to few men to become legends in their own lifetime. Superintendent John McLaren achieved that stature. A man of unique dimensions, he was a specialist in many areas which are separate departments today. He was all of them rolled into one—arborealist, floriculturist, botanist, landscapist, biologist, fertilizer expert—everything! He was Boss Gardener. And the sphere of his life's work is still there for all to see, a much-loved place, the city's greatest jewel. Through his genius, Golden Gate Park became, not a world of hodgepodge, but one of balance, harmony, and symmetry.

8   The Elements So Mixed

Geoffrey Studdert Kennedy, the chaplain-poet of the First World War, once described man as "a mixture" from "his head to the soles of his feet." John McLaren, like the rest of us, was a mixture of conflicting forces—sometimes arrogant, sometimes humble; sometimes patient, sometimes not; a grey-eyed dreamer of impossible dreams, and yet a down-to-earth realist with his feet firmly planted on terra firma. Like Shakespeare's Brutus "the elements were mixed in him." No one is all of a piece and John McLaren was certainly a man with many sides to his nature. It is this that makes him so interesting as a psychological study. He was a man larger than life.

John McLaren had an autocratic side to his nature which made him a hard man to work for. A human dynamo himself, he expected everyone else to be the same. As Boss Gardener, he wielded large and royal powers. He had high work-standards and ruthlessly demanded their observance. Woe betide the the man who fell short! A gardener would be summarily dismissed for smoking on the job or for wearing gloves while weeding. And yet, he was also a man of great humanity. If the breadwinner fell sick, he would hire another member of the family to take his place in order that the family should not be in want. And, strangely enough, drunkenness did not seem to count. "Take him home, and let him sleep it off," he would order. (Perhaps, like Burns, he felt that "to step aside is human.")

Superintendent McLaren also had a fetish about punctuality and an immense dislike for the faineant and lazy. His men well-nigh feared him. "Wild Game coming," they would signal whenever McLaren appeared on the horizon. It was their secret warning (like the schoolboy's 'Cave') to "look out" as the Old Man was coming.

Although a martinet, he was scrupulously fair. A thirty-third degree Mason, he "met upon the level and parted on the square." His nephew Peter Girvan, his sister Margaret's son, came out from Scotland to work for him, but the blood-bond made no difference. The Boss Gardener was just as hard on Peter as on any other workman. Peter soon left, not because of the work required of him, but because he disliked crowds and cities.

If McLaren drove his men relentlessly, he was equally hard on himself. Up each day at the crack of dawn, he would be in his office punctually at seven to give his fifty or more foremen their orders for the day—and sometimes in pretty plain terms. Often they would emerge seething with rage, having been given a drubbing for their previous day's performance. His mornings were normally spent in the office attending to the necessary paperwork, replying to correspondence, writing to experts throughout the world for seeds, placing orders for equipment, supplies, and so on. In the afternoons he would ride, or later, be driven (he couldn't drive, so was given a chauffeur) round the various parks of the city to oversee and inspect the work being done, all the while dreaming his dreams and seeing his visions of future projects. He spent as much time outside as possible. "Superintending is not an office job," he would say. He lived and breathed his work. Even when mixing the French dressing at the dining table before his evening meal, his thoughts were outside with the trees, flowers, birds and the weather. His men respected him. They knew that, although he was a hard taskmaster, he was fair and knew his job. McLaren had a great respect for what today is called "the working man," although that is a phrase he would not have used. To him, all men were working men, whatever their job or profession. He would not have made the sociological distinction.

John McLaren was extremely nimble-minded. Unable to drive, the Board provided a chauffeur for him, at $100 a month, till such time as McLaren could master the art of the steering wheel. After some years, the complaint was made that the Superintendent had not yet learned to drive. McLaren was non-plussed. He said he would learn to drive straightaway and, getting into the automobile, drove it into the nearest lake! The question was never again raised, and a driver was provided for the rest of his life.

Superintendent McLaren was a perfectionist. One day a man was planting shrubs. McLaren, over seventy at the time, watched for a moment or two, and then growled, "Move over," plucking the trowel from the man's nervous hand. "He put more plants in in ten minutes," said the workman, "than I put in in two hours. But that wasn't his complaint. His complaint was that I was holding the trowel the wrong way, with my thumb down the side of the handle, instead of down the front."

He was fiesty and a "bonnie fetcher," and the affairs of the Park were ever on his mind. The best interests of the Park were, to him, of overmastering importance. It was proposed that a streetcar line be laid in the Park. The suggestion aroused McLaren to raging fury. They were treading not only on his territory, but also on his corns and so, primed for battle, he stormed into the Railroad Office. "You can't lay a track there," he thundered. "You'll ruin the trees." It was pointed out to him that, according to the map, there were no trees in the area proposed. "Then your map's wrong," he shot back with Promethean fire. "That's where the rhododendrons are." Truth was there wasn't a single rhododendron in sight, but McLaren was determined that no track would be laid anywhere in the Park. It was agreed that the planners would visit the area the next day to inspect the site. All that night McLaren had his gardeners planting rhododendrons, and when the engineers arrived in the morning they beheld a resplendent field of color and abandoned their ill-starred scheme. "Go home now and get some sleep," said the Boss Gardener to his work-weary crew with an impish wink. He could be conniving and devious when the Park's best interest were at stake. To dismember the Park with a streetcar line was, in McLaren's eyes, unforgivable barbarity.

Another oft-told tale illustrating McLaren's intractable determination has to do with an oak tree. The Chief of Park Police asked Superintendent McLaren to remove an oak which was overshadowing the Station. "We'll compromise," suggested the stubborn ("thrawn" is the Scots word) Scot, "You move your Station." The tree remained. When asked later about the little contretemps, McLaren replied disarmingly, "Oh, it was just a wee misunderstandin'." McLaren would not destroy a tree unless it was absolutely necessary to do so and overshadowing a Police Station was insufficient reason. "I have no love for dead trees," he once said when a lady invited his admiration for a bedecked Christmas tree, "only for live ones"—and turned his back! It is an insight we would do well to ponder. McLaren would frown upon the modern practise of growing trees for Christmas decoration. To him, it would be like rearing pheasants for shooting— reprehensible! Like Dr. Schweitzer he loved living things and beauty, and sought always to serve Nature, life's great controlling power. Once a lady was visiting him in his office on her way to the country. As she said good-bye and turned toward the door he called her back. "Wait a minute," he said, reaching into a drawer. He drew out a little packet of wildflower seeds and handed them to her. "Take these with you to scatter about as you drive through the hills."

When the oak trees on the campus of the University of California were apparently dying of some mysterious ailment which defied the analysis of the professors, John McLaren, after one look at the ailing trees said, "They need nourishment. Feed them up. Treat them as you would a sick horse or cow. Dig trenches to the roots, following the course of the main limbs and give them fresh soil and leaf mold." After this treatment, the oaks recovered.

Once the "rascals down at City Hall" planned to extend a street through part of the Park—a plan with which the Superintendent was in ardent disagreement. Immediately he offered the land in question to the Police Department for a Training Academy. The offer was accepted and again the Park was saved. Better a Police Academy than a thoroughfare of screaming cars and blinking traffic lights!

McLaren's supreme achievement was keeping politics and commercialism out of the Park. "You look after the politics," he would say, "and I'll look after the parks." His sword could be sharp. He was determined that the parks would be for the relaxation and enjoyment of the people of San Francisco and not for political maneuvering or economic gain. No hot-dog stands and no charge for sports, if he could prevent it! Nature conservancy and quality of life were his overpowering aim, and this philosophy prevailed as long as he lived. That is why he was alienated and disliked by politicians, and why he was loved and supported by the San Franciscan people. Vested interests were at stake, but McLaren had great horticultural integrity.

John McLaren had a special love for children. One of his favorite spots in Golden Gate Park was the Children's Playground. One Easter Sunday, not long before he died, "Uncle John" (as everyone in San Francisco now called him) was visiting it with a friend. "When I came here first," reminisced the frail, old war-horse, "the wee ones had no place to play or make a maypole, or roll an Easter egg. Now, just look at them." The place was alive with children, hundreds of them, all laughing and happy, and that made John McLaren happy too. If he rejoiced in anything, it was in the joy and health and happiness that the parks had brought to the young. There were

Mr. and Mrs. John McLaren.

few "Keep Off the Grass" signs in Golden Gate Park. "I'd as soon think of keeping them off the tennis courts or out o' the ball park."

In 1906, after the earthquake, the Park became a refuge for the homeless. The schools also suffered in the disaster and classes were held al fresco in the Park. To each child, "Uncle John" allotted a small garden, ten feet square, in which he or she might grow vegetables. The children would ask, "How do you make things grow?" "The secret of making things grow," he would reply with a laugh, "is to keep their toes warm," and then he would show them how to do it. After the earthquake, Superintendent and Mrs. McLaren were thanked in an official resolution for the "magnificent and efficient manner in which assistance was rendered by them to the homeless who had applied for food and shelter at the Lodge during the days following the great conflagration."

McLaren enjoyed a remarkable and immense popularity with the people of San Francisco. Gertrude Atherton, in *My San Francisco,* says he was "perhaps the best-loved man in San Francisco." This was due, partly at least, to the Park he had created. Once a bleak, threatening wasteland where it was unsafe to travel, it had become a world-celebrated paradise. Men no longer feared the thief and the robber. Property values soared and people do not quarrel with prosperity. Also, McLaren had demonstrated that one man CAN fight City Hall—and win! He fearlessly confronted grafting bosses and dishonest mayors (at least one of whom ended up in San Quentin). That too, tends to make a man something of a hero. People like to see the "attics" (as Lloyd George used to call them, the "high-ups") get their come-uppance. McLaren fought a constant battle against political shenanigans. He refused to let politicians pay their political debts by padding park payrolls and refused also to tell his fellow-workers how they must vote and how they must not. That too, appeals to the public conscience. Above all McLaren loved children, and the quickest way to a parent's heart is through his child. All of these, together with the support he was given by the fraternal bodies to which he belonged (the Masonic Order, the Oddfellows, the Caledonian Society, etc.), provided a strong political base. I do not think he ever encountered popular opposition because he, himself, was the ultimate politician. His tentacles were wide-ranging.

Once, when two powerful politicians, out to build their empire, were seeking to railroad him out of office, a group of concerned friends called at the Lodge to discuss the matter. They found McLaren with a cool head, serene, composed, and with a firm hold on reality. "The people of San Francisco are my employers," he said in measured tones, "not the politicians at City Hall. If my work is satisfactory, the people will not permit an injustice and, if it is not satisfactory, if I do not deserve the confidence of those I have served, it is time I was asked to leave. Should the people fail to speak when corrupt interests seek to discredit me, then I shall take their silence as a request to step down." Before the day was over, the San Franciscans spoke loudly and clearly, and the conniving politicos were roundly defeated. Haman was hanged on the gallows he built for Mordecai! "Do the best you can," was John McLaren's philosophy, "and things will come out alright in the end and, even if they don't, if you've done your best, why then...," and there he let the matter rest. He knew that if he did his best he could trust the people. No matter how difficult or tense a situation, he refused to lie awake at night or to sicken himself with worry.

So great was Superintendent McLaren's popular appeal that when he reached the age of seventy in 1916 and was required, by city statute, to retire, the citizenry protested with such vehemence and devotion that an exception was made and the statute was changed, giving him life-tenure as Parks Superintendent at an increased salary. "I'm very glad," he said. "Not for the money which I do not need [McLaren was good with money, and knew the secret of making it grow], but for the time it will give

Jean Finlayson ("Wee Jeannie"), age nine.

me to do a lot of work I have planned." He lived for twenty-five more productive years.

"Uncle John" liked his glass of Scotch. Jean Finlayson, his goddaughter, who knew him better than most, writes: "When he came in at 5:00, he would make for the cabinet, pour himself a glass of

Scotch, his standard tipple, carry it to the living room where Maggie, the housekeeper, had his slippers waiting by his chair beside the fireplace. There, he would stretch out and relax with his newspaper until his evening meal was served, promptly at 6:00. He never overdrank."

In later life, when he came in in the evening, Matie's three small children would take turns unlacing his hooked boots for which each received a dime. All this, while he sipped his Scotch and read his paper.

In the summer of 1910, John McLaren was the subject of an enquiry for alleged malfeasance in office. A man in public office is always in danger of such charges being brought and they are very often brought by those who seek his job. The charge levelled against him was that he was giving special favors to a contracting company by allowing the company to use Park rock and sand for work they were doing on a city street. This, of course, would have been a misuse of Park property. His calumniators further alleged that the contractor in question was selling some of the sand to private citizens, and with McLaren's knowledge. McLaren's rebuttal was that he had made the agreement with the contractor (with the knowledge and authority of a former Park Board of Commissioners) in return for the free use of a score of the company's dumping carts for work in the Park. The matter was never resolved in any court and, therefore, it will never be known whether the charges made were spurious or real, trumped up or genuine. Truth is elusive. If McLaren was guilty of malfeasance (and there is certainly no such proof. There seems to be something almost too calculated about it.), I am sure it was not for personal financial gain, but rather for the benefit of Golden Gate Park.

John McLaren was a religious man, and could be seen in Westminster Presbyterian Church most Sundays, sometimes walking there (peppermints in pocket) along the Panhandle with Matie, his granddaughter, Jeannie Finlayson, his goddaughter (wearing their long white gloves and pretty, ribboned

Jane Mill with Matie, her granddaughter.

bonnets), and Maggie Miller, the housekeeper, while sometimes being driven there by his chauffeur, Edward Smith. When they reached the Presbyterian Church, Maggie would leave them, departing for her own Roman Catholic Chapel, there to keep the faith once delivered to her saints. In later years, Jane McLaren did not attend church services much, perhaps because she was over-conscious of her lameness rather than from apostasy. John always tried to go. In the peace of the church and its worship, he resolved "life's contraries" and caught, perhaps, a glimpse of the higher mysteries as his father and mother had done before him.

After Sunday lunch in the large dining room, he would go for a drive to inspect some park project that was under way, making notes of points he wished to remember, or of things he wanted done, all the while growling at the innocent Ed Smith, the chauffeur, who had nothing whatsoever to do with whatever it was that was displeasing him. Ed understood the old man perfectly, and so could cope. He was a loyal and likeable servant.

Such and more, much more, was John McLaren— a conjunction of influences and moods. Some of his foibles and ways he owed, no doubt, to his "genes" (which we used to call "blood"), others were peculiarly his own but, with them all, he was Studdert Kennedy's "mixture," and stubbornly Scottish, as Scotch as heather, and untamable. What faults he had were really all on the surface and they "leaned to virtue's side."

9   A Little Night Music

The attractive and commodious Romanesque building, known today as McLaren Lodge, serves as the Park offices and houses a large and varied staff of people. Originally, it was the home of John and Jane McLaren and part of it served also as Superintendent McLaren's office. (I still have the account rendered by the W. and J. Sloane Co. of 641-647 Market Street, dated May 15, 1896, for furnishings supplied when the McLarens moved in. It amounts to $7,522, a considerable sum in those days.)

At the beginning of the century, in the happy, carefree days before the First World War, when "all the lights went out," the Lodge was the center of a rich social and cultural life. Most notables visiting the city eventually ended up there. To Sir Harry Lauder, the music-hall star, the Lodge was a second home. An old photograph, taken before the earthquake, shows Sir Harry and Lady Lauder driving in an automobile with John and Jane McLaren, the ladies wrapped in Valenciennes lace and the men wearing the tricky little bowler hats which were the fashion of the time. Whenever Sir Harry was in San Francisco, he and John McLaren would spend a happy hour walking in the Park after dinner. And so with Lipton. All were good friends.

Musical evenings at the Lodge were common. The Robert Burns Society, of which McLaren was an ardent member, frequently met there to sing the poet's songs late into the night. McLaren's great-granddaughter, now living in Virginia, still remembers how she and her brothers, as children,

The present Lodge, built in 1895.

used to sit at the top of the stairs listening to the bacchanalian sounds of revelry emanating from the smoke-filled drawing-room below.

Post-performance soirees were also held from time to time at which world-famous artists would delight Lodge guests with their virtuosity. To these musical evenings the city's leading politicians and influential and wealthy citizens would be regularly invited, for McLaren and the Park Commissioners were always in need of funds for Park projects and this was one profitable way of getting them. On such occasions, the

Lodge "stank with Excellencies," as they used to say of Princess Metternich's sparkling European receptions.

Merola and the Opera Singers were frequent guests. Margaret Geddes tells of one of their visits. Merola asked McLaren how he had enjoyed the opera beforehand. "Not at all," responded the straight-forward little Scot. "I don't understand opera and I'm tired of those Russian Rhapsodies, Italian Arpeggios, and Spanish Serenades. Give me some wholesome music like 'The Yellow Rose of Texas'." "Where can I find the score?" Merola asked. "Don't ask me," shot back McLaren, "I'm a gardener, not a musician. I don't ask you where I can find a certain tree, do I?" It was all pleasant, good-natured banter between friends.

Enrico Caruso also sang there—and big-bosomed Luisa Tetrazzini, and Mary Garden who captivated everyone with her saucy insouciance. Immortal names! Caruso, Tertazzini, Garden! "Olympus' faded hierarchy!"

> Alas! Those noble beings are no more;
> They have left enduring moments.

Caruso, with his soaring, glorious tenor, could fill any concert hall in the world and sang in San Francisco on the eve of the earthquake. Maybe even at the Lodge in Golden Gate afterwards. It is not only a possibility, but a probability for he sang there several times.

Tetrazzini was one of the best coloratura sopranos of all time, if only because there have been so few of them. Hers was a magnificent, powerful voice, beyond superlatives, and it was in great demand in both Europe and America. Luisa Tetrazzini was an enormous and superb talent, her voice rich and powerful. How the Lodge must have echoed and re-echoed to the strains of her "Tannhauser" and German lieder!

Mary Garden was McLaren's favorite, if only because she was a fellow-Scot who hailed from Aberdeen. A pupil of the renowned Madame

Marchese, she later became the friend and protege of Debussy who composed his "Pelleas et Melissande" especially for her. She was the first in the world to sing the part of Melissande and she did so beautifully. Like Tetrazzini, she had a voice of great range and power, and when she sang the "auld Scots sangs"— "Roman Tree" or "O, Whistle and I'll Come to You, My Lad"—the Boss Gardener, Scots to the bone, would applaud loudly. "Far better than all that opera nonsense," he would comment with impish glee and in his broad Scots accent. Mary Garden lived into her nineties and died in Inverurie, not far from where she had been born. I once heard her in the sixties, an old woman, her singing days long done, being interviewed on the B.B.C. She spoke of her career, her friendships, her philosophy, of many things. Soon afterwards she died.

The accompanist at these Lodge ensembles at one time was Jeannie Finlayson, a most talented musician and virtuoso of piano, violin, and mandolin. Her husband, Tom, was a young Scottish architect, trained in Glasgow, who had come to San Francisco in 1907, to work on the rebuilding of the city after the earthquake and fire. He had arrived bearing a letter of introduction to Superintendent John McLaren from the McLaren family back home in Muirside, Bannockburn. His fiancee, Jeannie Brooks Youll came out to join him later as his bride and the young couple stayed at the Lodge for a short time where they were welcome and popular guests. Tom Finlayson, like his young wife, was a great lover of music and the possessor of a fine, rich basso. He and his young bride contributed much to these happy, carefree evenings long ago, when the McLarens and their guests enjoyed "A Little Night Music." A vanished age of gaiety, grace, and charm, though I suspect the Boss Gardener must have grown a little weary sometimes of the operatic torture. He was not without culture, but it lay in other directions!

Jeannie, the young wife, died from the endemic typhoid which struck the city in 1910, less than three years after her marriage, when her little baby

Jean Finlayson Holmes.

daughter was only two weeks old. Her young husband was devastated. He had loved her dearly, and she had returned his love in the fullest measure. The McLarens' chauffeur, Edward Smith, collected the babe from the Children's Hospital and took her to the nursery at the Lodge where was another motherless child, Matie, the McLarens' granddaughter, whose mother (their son Donald's wife), had died three years earlier in childbirth. A crib was set up in the nursery for "Wee Jeannie," as the new baby was called, and she was cared for by the faithful Maggie Miller, the housekeeper. Wee Jeannie's crib soon became the center of attention and attraction and she was loved and cared for till her broken-hearted father could make other arrangements.

When Wee Jeannie was baptized, John and Jane McLaren were her godparents and she always remained an important part of the McLaren family. Matie and she grew up together, like sisters, and their fidelity to each other spanned the years. Their friendship ended only with Matie's death in 1967 at the age of sixty.

A foster-mother was eventually found, but Wee Jeannie spent every weekend at the Lodge with "Grandma and Grandpa" and Matie. Matie and she were always dressed alike, the dressmaker being instructed by Mrs. McLaren to make two of everything, and both wore gold lockets round their necks encasing pictures of their lost mothers.

On what turned out to be her last visit to the Lodge, her first home, Wee Jeannie, a grown, married woman, found John McLaren bed-ridden and vague, but "he took my hand," she writes. "I sat on the bed beside him and put my hand on his chest. He smiled, hugged me and patted me but said nothing. He didn't have to." In a letter I once received from her she confides, "Your Aunt Jane and Uncle John never made me feel unwanted or a nuisance. Maybe that is why I loved them so." John McLaren "gave her away" on her wedding day, and Matie was her bridesmaid.

Matie, who became Mrs. Daniels, bore three children. A graduate of Stanford, she had a rare and remarkable mind with an enormous interest in history. She was a talented pianist, specializing in Chopin, and an accomplished artist in both oils and watercolors. She painted beautiful things. She was also a poet of no mean merit, and as a student at Stanford, had excelled as an athlete, a hurdler. Dorothea Lange, the noted photographer of the Depression years, was a close friend and her neighbor in North Beach, the artists' section of San Francisco in the 1930s. (Miss Lange took a very striking portrait of Matie just before her marriage.) Matie McLaren Daniels died from a brain tumor which, undiagnosed, had caused her much intense pain and suffering throughout a large part of her life. My mother often spoke of the intense, searing headaches which used to affect her even as a teen-ager on vacation in Scotland.

Wee Jeannie, continued to write, paint, and tend her beloved flowers, until her death on October 28, 1987 in Larkspur, California.

10   Sorrow's Crown of Sorrow

The great sorrow of John and Jane McLaren's life was the tragic and unexpected death of their son Donald. "This is a terrible thing that has stricken us," was McLaren's stunned comment upon learning of the death in the early morning hours of a day in June 1925. He never again referred to it publicly. Donald was only forty-six and mystery still surrounds his passing.

Donald McLaren was someone special but the happiness he sought eluded him. As a boy he was athletic and lissome, sociable and attractive, entirely charming with endless desirable qualities. His dream growing up was to be a baseball player but parental direction dictated otherwise and he became, instead, a landscape gardener like his father. He was skilled as such, and prospered. Nevertheless, throughout his life he remained a frustrated baseball player.

Donald had a happy boyhood and youth and was popular with his companions. He was intelligent and bright and whether vacationing with his parents in the remote resort at Mt. Herman, swimming in the river there (his father laughingly chasing the water snakes away), or walking in the Sierras on weekend trips, sleeping round a campfire on a bedroll, he entered life enthusiastically.

On the completion of high school, he enrolled in the University of California at Berkeley from which he graduated in timely fashion and with a good degree, and where he also played baseball, a game in which he greatly excelled. Ultimately, he became partner and co-owner of the McRorie-McLaren

Donald McLaren, age 8.

Nursery in San Mateo, a successful and efficient business concern. He married Miss Martha Leonard, a well-to-do merchant's daughter from Berkeley who, judging by her picture, must have been rather beautiful, with her ribboned hair and soft, dark eyes. Theirs was a solid union and they were extremely happy, but, alas, only for a short while. Sorrow struck when Martha died in childbirth and Donald was left with his little baby daughter, Matie, whom he grew to love dearly. He never overcame Martha's death.

Some years later, he married a lady named Helen, but I don't think the marriage was entirely happy, though I do not know this for a fact. Little Matie worshipped her father, but never quite took to her new mother (and obstinately refused to call her such), and continued to live at the Lodge with her grandparents.

Matie was the apple of her father's eye, and he was an excellent father to her. He spoiled her unashamedly. He would sweep her up in his arms and, full of fun, whirl her, making her scream with gales of laughter, to the ceiling. Sometimes he, Matie, and Wee Jeannie would visit the movie theater where Donald would unfailingly indulge them with a huge box of delicious chocolates. He was an indulgent, devoted father, always happy and filled with infectious gaiety.

When his business partner died, the full weight of the Nursery fell upon Donald's shoulders. This resulted in overwork with little time for rest and relaxation. More and more he sought solace in the bottle until, finally, John Barleycorn totally consumed him and he became a "problem drinker," an alcoholic. In those days, there was no place to turn to for help, no support groups or Alcoholics Anonymous, no agencies for long-term therapy. His was a battle he had to wage alone and victory eluded him.

At the time of his death he was engaged, according to newspaper reports, in an important contract with the Reno Exposition Company in Nevada, a venture which demanded much time and energy. After spending some days in that city, working hard and late, he returned to San Francisco utterly worn and spent. All he desired was a "quiet hotel where I can rest." A cab driver drove him to the Alp Rose, an establishment in the Mission district of the city and there, one night at midnight, he was found dead in bed with the gas-burner turned on but unlit. At the ensuing inquest, the coroner's verdict was pronounced "Suicide Brought On By Overwork." And there the matter ended. It seemed a reasonable conclusion.

Maggie Miller, faithful servant that she was, could not bring herself to accept the verdict, and consistently and persistently refused to do so. "I knew Donald," she would say with sadness in her eyes, "and he never committed suicide." Her theory, I think, was that he may have put a coffee-pot on the burner which later boiled over, extinguished the flame, and Donald, asleep in his weariness, was unaware of the escaping gas and consequently perished. Suicide or accidental death or something else, we shall never know. The mystery remains, but whatever the cause, his death was a great sorrow. His youthful promise had been great but things, somewhere, went wrong. Who knows what?

> One point must still be greatly dark,
>   The moving WHY they do it:
> And, just as lamely can ye mark
>   How far perhaps they rue it.
> Who made the heart, 'tis He alone
>   Decidedly can try us;
> He knows each chord—its various tone,
>   Each spring—its various bias:
> Then, at the balance, let's be mute,
>   We never can adjust it;
> What's done we partly may compute,
>   But know not what's resisted.

To Matie, the shock of her father's death came like the end of the world, causing her extreme distress and anguish. On the night he died, she, a happy, carefree sixteen-year-old, was entertaining some of her Lowell High School friends at a celebration of some kind in

Martha Leonard McLaren, age 8.

Martha Leonard (top) with her sisters.

the Palace Hotel. It had been a happy time, completely
so, and then, in the morning of a bright and beautiful
day she read the headline, "McLaren Dies By Suicide."
She was crushed beyond consolation and an
emotional shock, like a great sweeping wind, set in
and from it she never completely recovered.   It
overshadowed, like a dark storm-cloud, the remainder
of her life.

Donald's death probably hastened his mother's

passing. Jane's whole life-style changed. She withdrew from public life to live in grief-stricken seclusion at the Lodge. The afternoon teas which she had served each day with such grace to varied guests—a gardener's grieving widow, a titled lady, a famous actress—all stopped, as did her charitable and philanthropic works and her sympathy for noble causes. Her husband kept hoping that she might be able to pick up the threads and gather strength enough to attain the light again, but such hopes were vain and, after some fifteen months, a few weeks after observing her Golden Wedding, the "bugle blew reveille to the breaking morn" and she passed gently into life eternal at the Lodge, the place which had been her home for forty years. "Her beauty and charm," wrote Margaret Geddes, the secretary, "endeared her to everyone but now her voice is stilled, as is Donald's." Her marriage fifty years earlier had attracted no attention. Her death was given national prominence, being widely and sorrowfully reported.

Thus in the space of two years John McLaren had lost the two people who meant most to him in life. Donald had helped him plan the Panama-Pacific International Exposition, and other projects, which had received world-wide acclaim a few short years before. But, somewhere, sometime, somehow, something went wrong and Donald, the once splendid young man, "the gilded youth," lost his way. To live in the shadow of a famous father so completely in control of himself must have been difficult for him, and the death of his young wife in the moment of a woman's greatest joy, must have cut deep. These, together with the pressures and demands of a growing business, may have driven him to the bottle and premature grave. But it must also be said, with appropriate charity, that Donald lacked his father's ambition and strength and never fully developed his own undoubted talents.

The loss of wife and son told heavily upon the aging John McLaren, though he chose not to show his personal sorrow. Friends gathered round to strengthen and support, and their efforts to sustain were filled

With Matie McLaren Daniels, her husband, and children.

with fortifying grace but, even so, the strain proved too burdensome and in the early spring of the following year, 1927, he became gravely ill. Three nurses were in attendance at the Lodge around the clock. A team of doctors and specialists was called in but, seemingly, to no avail and it was reported in the press that John McLaren, the "genius of Golden Gate," lay near to death. Nevertheless, the resilient Scot, small in stature but of giant heart, weathered the storm and, with great supremacy of spirit, recovered to live for seventeen more productive years, driving himself relentlessly, "aye stickin' in a tree," and continuing, grey-eyed dreamer that he was, with his plans for Golden Gate and the other city parks. Like Camus, he "seemed to carry inside himself an invincible summer in life's dark winter." That he did so was due to the fact that he had work to do and work became his savior and anchor of stability in his seemingly disintegrating world. He adhered rigidly to his formula, "aye keep busy." That had always been his dictum and he continued to observe it during the years that yet remained. And, of course, there still was Matie, the parentless teenager, his granddaughter, who needed him. The two grew close. Sometimes he would take her to the Ice Follies, sometimes to the Manger, his favorite restaurant, where, as soon as he sat down, the waiter would appear with a bowl of his favorite soup—French onion with Parmesan cheese. Now a student at Stanford University, Matie became his special care and joy. Later, after she married, her children brought endless comfort to him in his declining years.

11 Points of Honor

A surfeit of honors came to John McLaren and they brought him great pleasure. Dinners and receptions given by his fellow-citizens in tribute were not an infrequent occurrence. In December 1935, for example, the Rose Bowl of the Palace Hotel in San Francisco was filled to overflowing, many people having to stand, thick as sardines, round the edges, jostling one another, because all available seats had been taken. Pipe-music filled the room and Scots songs were sung, bringing tears to the old gardener's failing eyes. Speakers salted their orations with such accolades as "San Francisco's First Citizen," her "Fourth Dimension," and the "Man Who Made Nature His Handmaiden." The praise was over-generous perhaps, but it was sincerely given and was typical of the affection in which the people held him. Asked at the end of the proceedings to say a few words, the old man issued his stock reply, "I think I am not gifted that way." Such receptions were an almost annual event.

McLaren was held in great esteem by his professional peers as well. In 1939, he was appointed a delegate to the Annual Convention of Park Executives in Philadelphia. It was his first plane trip and Matie went with him. A newspaper reported at the time:

McLaren on Plane

Because he "doesn't believe in being old-fashioned," 93-year-old John McLaren, creator of San Francisco's Golden Gate Park, left by plane yesterday to attend the Park Superintendents' national convention in Philadelphia. With him, as he boarded a United Airlines mainliner for his first air trip were a grandchild, Mrs. Joseph Daniels, and her husband. Rules banning cigars en route were waived for Mr. McLaren.

When he arrived, he was presented with a citation signed by seventy-eight members of the American Institute of Park Executives. It is a lengthy document, too long to reproduce in full, but part of it reads:

To: JOHN MCLAREN, our Honorary member and Venerable Dean at the Fortieth Convention of the American Institute of Park Executives, Philadelphia, Nineteen Thirty Nine.

We, the members of the American Institute of Park Executives, meeting at the Fortieth annual convention, at Philadelphia, Pennsylvania, on the twentieth day of September, 1939, SALUTE on the occasion of his ninety third year, our Dean and Eminent Leader, John McLaren...appointed Superintendent of Parks of San Francisco in April of eighteen hundred and eighty seven; harnessing the forces of the sea waves and winds to build protective dykes and lands; to enliven the winds of picturesque windmills that lift sweet waters from the Earth to feed lagoons, streams and waterfalls and to produce and sustain plant life; transforming Yerba Buena's desolate sand dunes into the luxuriantly verdant crown of San Francisco's Golden Gate; serving the public weal zealously, inspiredly, over half a century...We revere the accomplishments of John McLaren; his outstanding record of

service to his devotedly grateful San
Francisco...; his merited position,
internationally accorded, or America's
leading Park Man, Landscape Gardener and
Plant Man; his exemplification of the public
servant...; his holding steadfastly through
life to his father's advice: "When at a loss
for something to do, plant a tree," and
relaying that precept to other generations in
another land....

An outstanding tribute from fellow-gardeners and
horticulturists! McLaren was respected by his peers for
his professionalism, horticultural knowledge, and
magnificent contribution to his calling.

The highest award John McLaren received was an
Honorary Doctorate of Laws (LL.D) from the
University of California. This was bestowed in 1931
and the citation, reminiscent of Sir Christopher
Wren's at St. Paul's Cathedral, reads, "John McLaren,
beloved of the people of the entire State, doughty
champion of beauty in city planning, his alchemy
transformed the shifting sands by the Pacific into the
loveliness of trees and flowers. Of him it may be truly
said, as one stands in Golden Gate Park, 'If you would
seek his monument, look about you'." Dougal, his
cairn terrier, (the "brawest wee dog in the world," and
as ken-speckled in the city as his master) sat quietly at
his feet during the conferral of the degree at Berkeley.
For days afterwards, the Lodge was inundated with a
flood of congratulatory mail addressed to "Dr. John
McLaren." He felt very proud.

Some years earlier, in 1923, McLaren had received
the George Robert White Medal of Honor from the
Massachusetts Horticultural Society, for "eminence in
horticultural achievement." The medal of coin gold
weighs some eight-and-one-half ounces and is the
supreme award of its kind in the country. Over the
years it has been given to some highly distinguished
recipients the world over. The first recipient in 1909
(the year of its inception) was Professor Charles S.
Sargent. Some others have been Frederick Law

McLaren, right, with unidentified man.

Olmsted (1937), Sir Arthur William Hill, of Kew Gardens (1940), Lord Aberconway, London Horticultural Society (1948), Sir William Wright Smith of the Edinburgh Botanical Gardens (1951), and the most recent recipient, Dr. Peter Raven (1987), Director of the Missouri Botanical Garden and Professor of Botany at Washington University, St. Louis, Missouri.

McLaren won the Medal in 1923, fourteen years before Olmsted, and the Massachusetts Horticultural Society's Year Book for that year reads:

> At the age of 17, young McLaren took up the study of landscape gardening. His first training school was the Scotch farm of his parents. After serving a long apprenticeship at the Edinburgh Botanical Garden he set out for California and came first to San Mateo, where he resided for a number of years, and planted the large eucalyptus and pines now growing along the highway and in private grounds....McLaren, upon taking charge of the Park, found himself in possession of a newly-planted strip of land, the Panhandle, a conservatory and many acres of sand. There were no lakes and few would have considered them a possibility. The story of John McLaren's life and works since that time is written in a book that he who runs may read. The Children's Playground, the Concert Pavilion, Strawberry Hill with Stow Lake and Huntington Falls, the Chain of Lakes and the flora of many lands are among its chapters. It is painted in colors that surpass any words of description. It was John McLaren who performed much of the wizardry that caused the Marina to spring suddenly into beautiful gardens as a setting for the Panama-Pacific Exposition.... McLaren is both author and authority. His

Pen and Ink drawing of McLaren by Matie, his granddaughter.

book, *Gardening in California: Landscape and Flower,* is the best in its field....

In 1930, Superintendent McLaren was created an Associate of Honor of the Royal Horticultural Society of England, being only the thirty-first recipient to receive that distinction since the Society's inception in

1804. All of these were considerable honors from prestigious institutions, reserved only for the elite, the most outstanding in their profession, and to receive them was glory indeed. John McLaren was proud to receive them.

But there were other honors, too, recognitions of a lesser nature. In 1927, one of the parks he himself had created in the southern hills overlooking the Bay, in Visitacion Valley, was named "John McLaren Park" in his honor and Mayor Rossi issued the following proclamation:

> Whereas John McLaren, beloved citizen of San Francisco has been honored in the naming of McLaren Park, and Whereas his work in planning this Park and other parks of the city during the past half century for the delight of our citizens has brought him high and wide world fame....Now, therefore, as Mayor of San Francisco, I hereby proclaim June 13th as annual John McLaren Day and, in the name of the city, I urge all citizens and especially the children, to join together at McLaren Park at one thirty p.m. to celebrate it fittingly.

Soon after, McLaren wrote a letter to his niece, my mother. The letter is edged with the black of mourning, the custom of the time, since Jane had died only a few months earlier.

> My Dear Niece,
>
> I have been kept very busy with a new park the City has just purchased. It contains 550 acres and the people of San Francisco have named it after your Uncle—the 'John McLaren Park.' We had a grand celebration. It seemed the whole city was there with procession of school children at least a mile long, with brass bands and

speeches by the Mayor and other
prominent citizens, all in my honor, so I
feel rather proud that they thought so much
of me that this tract will bear the McLaren
name. I enclose a copy of the programme
for the day. I am only sorry that poor Jane
was not spared to be with me that day.
Matie is still at Stanford and keeping up
with her studies very well. I hope you
will write to us soon again and let us know
how you all are. Matie and I often talk
about the good time you gave us when we
were home in dear old Scotland, the
pleasant times we had together singing the
sweet old songs and talking over old times
with your Mother etc. Kindly remember
us to all your friends. I am sorry I have
been so slow in answering your last letter
but I have been a little under the weather
and did not feel like writing but I am better
now and will try to do better in the future.
I had an attack of gall stones that pained me
very much and left me weak and lazy,
Kind regards to your Mother, Jimmy,
Donald, Miss Muirhead and the children
and with much love, I remain,

Your affectionate Uncle,
John McLaren

Of all the honors John McLaren received, none
gave him greater joy than a silver cup which was
presented to him by the children of San Francisco in
1915 at the time of the Panama-Pacific Exposition
which he had been asked to plan and direct, and
which was such a signal success. "I care more for that
than almost anything I've got," he once said. "It's
bigger than the Lipton Cup the big yachts race for.
Aye, and it's worth more. But it's not its value I care
for. It's the way I got it. It was brought for me by the
children of San Francisco and not one of them was

allowed to give more than ten cents." The inscription reads: "To Superintendent John McLaren—For the Sweetness and Gaiety of Blossoming Flowers that was his great contribution to the San Francisco Exposition." The cup was always given pride of place in the Lodge sitting room.

A rhododendron bears his name. It was developed by Mr. Eric Walther, the botanist at the Park and the man in charge of the Arboretum. Walther created the bloom by cross-fertilizing the early-flowering Cornubia (named after an oriental queen) with the Falconeri (named for Falconer, a Scottish financier). The latter, I think, had been sent to McLaren in the 1880s by his friend, Sir Joseph Hooker, Director of Kew Gardens in London. The John McLaren Rhododendron is scarlet and extremely beautiful—"a delight to the eyes," a writer described it. It is fitting that Eric Walther should have given his creation McLaren's name for the rhododendron was McLaren's favorite flower, and had been ever since his Edinburgh days at the Royal Botanic Gardens where it grows in rich profusion and for which the Gardens today are world-famous.

McLaren was also reproduced on canvas and in bronze, which I suppose might be regarded as an honor. Salvatore Cartaino Scarpitta, the Italian sculptor, resident of Hollywood, and creator of portraits of notable people, was commissioned to cast a life-size bust of John McLaren in bronze, and Earl Cummings sculptured a full-size statue of him which now stands in Golden Gate Park in the Memorial Rhododendron Dell. It is well–known that McLaren was against "stookies" (the Scots word) in the Park ("stookies and sequoias don't mix") but that was one battle he lost. There are many there but always he did his best to hide them. The statue, once placed, would be surrounded by obstructing plantings. His own statue was not placed in the Park until after his death, for he would not permit it there in his life-time. Indeed, he hid it under some trash in the stables! "The laddies aren't going to throw stones at me! There was a wee boy at our school who won high prestige among us because he knocked the neb [nose] off a stookie."

McLaren was also painted several times in oils. In 1921 Arthur Cahill, the San Francisco artist, was commissioned to paint his portrait and that work, presented on loan to the Park Commissioners by Mr. A. B. Spreckels, the sugar king and president of the San Mateo Electric Railway, now stands in the Commissioners Room at McLaren Lodge, what was once the dining room. William Barr, another noted artist in his day, also selected McLaren as a subject.

And there were other honors. A school was given his name, as was the Park Lodge after his death. He has been the subject of countless articles in countless publications and there have been parades in his honor without number. None of it he sought, for he was in reality a humble man. McLaren did not go out of his way to court the world and yet world recognition came to him. In serving Nature, the supreme controller of his life, he played his predestined part, ("I think I was born with the gift of being able to make things grow"), and as he did so, the world came to his door to acclaim his undoubted genius and acknowledge his leadership. As Raymond Clary has it in his *The Making of Golden Gate Park: The Growing Years,* "His memory will linger as long as there is a park in San Francisco." Mr. Clary also writes, on the same page, "We would do well to emulate his values today."

12 A Dios

John McLaren was a man of immense
dimensions and clear pragmatic vision. What he did,
he did well, and he died full of years and full of
honors. Towards the end he became extremely weak,
and it was clear that his life was ebbing away. The
vitality had gone, as had the fire of the war-horse
years. Debility crept in. But death held no terrors.
Timor mortis non conturbat me. His last years were
sad and lonely, but he bore the loneliness and waning
powers with the same stout heart with which he had
battled the sand and the sea half a lifetime earlier.

On January 1, 1943, New Year's Day, Wing
Commander Rossie Brown, a chaplain with the
Royal Air Force, happened to be in San Francisco for
the annual Shriner's football game. The game over,
his host drove him through Golden Gate Park, all the
while telling him its story. He spoke of "Uncle John,"
who had come there fifty-six years before and who
was now lying in the Lodge, sick unto death, having
been ill for some weeks. Chaplain Brown, a Scot from
Edinburgh, confided that he would like to call and see
McLaren, if that were possible. At the door of the
Lodge, the nurse admitted him, believing that his visit
would lift the old man's spirits. McLaren could no
longer speak but was in full possession of his mental
faculties.

Wing Commander Brown's kindness was beyond
words. He found the frail, shrunken, little gardener
sitting in his bedroom in a high window-seat
overlooking his beloved Park, "an impressive figure,
Napoleon-looking, whose eyes gleamed appraisingly at

me under his shaggy eyebrows."

"Mr. McLaren," he said, "I am a Scotsman, a minister from Edinburgh, and I've just come to wish you a Happy New Year, and to tell you that Scotland is proud of you and of this glorious park that you've created here." The old man could not reply, but he understood and seemed pleased.

In telling of the visit, Chaplain Brown remembered how he saw hanging on the wall, where the old man's eye could light upon it, a painting of a Scottish village. The nurse informed him that it had hung there ever since she had come. It was a picture of Bannockburn, the little village, where he had first seen the light of day almost a century before. As Chaplain Brown left the room, a soft look crept into the old man's eyes and the faint flicker of a smile touched his lips. As with Gilgamesh, "a mist of sleep, like soft wool, drifted over him." He turned his dewy eyes towards the window once again and one can only wonder what it was that he saw. The pines and deodars of Golden Gate silhouetted against the setting sun? Or did he see the Colonel's Wood where he had wandered as a boy? Or the Bannockburn with the wild rose bursting into radiant bloom on its grassy bank in June? Perhaps it was the corn, ripe unto harvest, swaying gently in the Muirside field in August? Did he hear again his father's voice beside the fire telling of the "Bonnie Prince" and the clansmen gathered round him at Culloden? Perhaps he thirsted for a quaigh (the Gaelic for a wooden drinking cup. I still have a quaigh McLaren's father carved from oak while a shepherd) of sweet, cold water from the well, thirty-foot deep, at the bottom of the Muirside garden? Great is the power of memory.

> From across the fields of yesterday,
>   He sometimes comes to me;
> A little boy just back from play—
>   The boy I used to be.

A few days later, on January 12, John McLaren died at 8:20 P.M. at the Lodge, his home on Stanyan

With Martha and John Daniels, his great-grandchildren.

Street, in his ninety-seventh year. He had suffered two strokes in a week, and was too ill to be removed to a hospital. Thus, his wish to die at home, surrounded by the things he loved, was granted. Outside his window were his masterpieces, the trees and the flowers he had planted, watered, and cared for. In his last illness he was given all possible care and kindness from his nurse, Agnes Ebeling, and her colleagues.

The following day his simple oak coffin, lying in a bed of heather, was placed in the Rotunda of the City Hall, his final honor. Hundreds, young and old, filed past in tribute to one who, for more than half a

century, had been part of their city and their lives. As
one writer put it, "The story of San Francisco is the
story of John McLaren. Both were young when they
first met." Time and time again, Eastern cities had
sought to lure him away with the promise of
glittering rewards but "he knew he was here to stay,"
as he had said when he first saw San Francisco.

After the lying in state, a funeral service was held
in the Masonic Temple on January 15, 1943. The Rev.
Dr. John Hays Creighton of the Presbyterian Church
read McLaren's favorite psalms and Superior Judge
Robert McWilliams delivered the eulogy in place of
Mr. John L. McNab, the McLaren family lawyer, and
friend of many years, who was ill. In his eulogy,
however, Judge McWilliams quoted part of an address
McNab had given four years earlier at a Caledonian
Society banquet:

> The annual pushes forth with Spring,
> blooms in the sunshine of the summertime,
> fades with autumn and dies with the
> winter snows. But the evergreen, with
> perennial hardihood, thrives through
> summer air and winter's frosts, a breath of
> immortality among flowers. So, tonight,
> we Scots gather to honor him whose
> noblest epitaph to be written, I hope many
> years from now, may read in words as
> simple as his life—
>
> 'Here honored of all the world, lies John
> McLaren, a Scottish gardener.'

John McLaren was buried in Cypress Lawn
Cemetery in Colma, beneath the shadow of San Bruno
Mountain, his grave marked with a chaste and simple
stone, like the one that marks his parents' grave in
Stirling.

On January 16, 1943, the day following the
funeral, the *San Francisco Chronicle* printed a beautiful
and moving account of "Uncle John's" last drive
through the Park he loved:

A Requiem of His Whispering Trees

The song of the sea was John McLaren's requiem yesterday...the song of the sea and the whisper of the wind as it drifted through the trees of Golden Gate Park.

This was the music he knew and loved, and this was the music he heard as he drove through the wooded mazes of his park for the last time.

The pilgrimage was ostensibly a procession of death. Yet as the cortege wound its way through the tree-framed glens, it became apparent that for John McLaren there was no death nor oblivion, but an immortality almost beyond understanding.

Uncle John was dead. But the work of his hands towers toward the sky, immutable, ageless, wrapped in the serene beauty of eternity.

Little knots of men and women stood silently along shaded lanes as the procession inched from Park Lodge, Uncle John's home, toward South Drive.

Children, sailing proud ships on lakes he had created for them, paused in their play, instinctively aware a trusted friend had come and gone.

All, somehow, was silent, there in the park. Even the great arms of the Dutch windmills seemed suspended and the rush of waterfalls was muted.

As the people of San Francisco paid Uncle John final tribute, so did his great masterpiece...the wonderland he built out of swirling sands and sage green brush.

There was no work yesterday in Golden Gate Park. The 400 gardeners, the men who toiled with Uncle John dropped their caps and overalls, and in their Sunday best, accompanied him to Cypress Lawn Cemetery where he was buried beside his wife and son.

To them, as to the millions who have loved his handiwork, Uncle John was the master—the boss gardener—who had given more than 50 of his 96 years that life in San Francisco might be more beautiful.

These were the men who accompanied Uncle John on his last tour of his park, past beds of sleeping azaleas and rhododendrons; past beds of purple violets and pansies. Winter wrapped them still in sleep but spring would awaken them to the glory planned by John McLaren.

The cortege of sleek dark cars and bouncing jalopies went on and on, along North Drive to the Great Highway at the ocean beach and over South Drive. Then it left the park and the pace increased and Uncle John's journey was nearly over.

A city ordinance was broken to permit Uncle John that final tour, but no one protested, since accompanying the boss gardener were the Mayor and members of the Park Commission and police and firemen and all the city officials whom Uncle John had battled over a lifetime to keep his parks beautiful.

So was the Master Gardener's body laid to rest in the place where, some seventeen years earlier, he had laid his wife and son. His work accomplished and his own day done, he joined them. A Dios.

Postscript

I have visited Golden Gate Park on five or six
occasions, and have always found each visit to be
more enjoyable and enlightening than the last. One
truth emerges abiding and sure—Superintendent John
McLaren left San Francisco a better and far more
beautiful city than he found it, and for that alone he
ought always to be gratefully remembered.

On my last visit, made in the autumn of 1987, I
was privileged to meet two former employees, now
retired—men who had worked for, and with, John
McLaren. The first of these was actually born in the
Park in a tent. His father, a Park employee before him,
had lost the family home in the earthquake and fire of
April 18, 1906, and with thousands of others, had set
up a makeshift abode in the grounds. In the tent set up
by the father, the son was born. On leaving school,
the boy joined the Park staff and never left it. He spent
his working years in Golden Gate. In the course of the
years, he rose to the position first, of foreman, and
then of Superintendent, an office which he carried
through with forcefulness, ability, and insight.

The second retiree had also spent a lifetime
working in the Park, ending his career there as
General Manager of the Recreation and Parks
Department. He too rendered signal service. That day
both reminisced and it was interesting for me, a great-
nephew of John McLaren, to listen in and hear them
speak of the Boss's foibles and (sometimes) funny
ways, his fierce battles with authority, and the heavy
demands he sometimes made upon his gardeners.
Both, however, seemed to respect his ability and the

strong stand he persistently and unfailingly took with regard to the Park's administration.

A few months earlier, I had attended the San Francisco Landscape Garden Show held at Fort Mason, and while there, was introduced to an old lady who never knew Superintendent McLaren, but who was somewhat less generous in her assessment of his qualities than were the two gentlemen. "I never knew him," said the bejeweled duchess, "but I am told that he was a bit of a curmudgeon." No doubt true. But sometimes, madam, a man has to be a curmudgeon if those around him are being invincibly stupid and woefully short-sighted and had not McLaren been difficult at times, a "bit of a curmudgeon," it might well be that San Francisco would not have the prodigiously splendid and dramatic heritage it enjoys today in Golden Gate Park, surely one of the world's most beautiful. A dedicated, single-minded, uncompromising man who knew his job, McLaren fought the infamies of "grafting bosses and dishonest mayors," as Gertrude Atherton puts it, and because of the unyielding stand he took, became "probably the best-loved man in San Francisco."

To maintain the parks of any city in these difficult days of severe financial cut-backs and reduced budgets must be incredibly hard and to preserve them from vandalism, in all its raging forms, well-nigh impossible. Voluntary groups, of course, step in to help raise funds and underwrite the necessary projects; nonetheless, the day-to-day administration must be, at times, an enormous nightmare.

One of the principle problems is the reduced number of gardening personnel available to meet the needs of the parks. There is no scarcity of office staff, but gardeners would appear to be harder to come by. Also, the endless requests to use the Park for baseball, softball, soccer, rugby, horseback riding, croquet, bicycle riding, volleyball, frisbee tossing, roller skating, and jogging has, in some areas, completely devastated and destroyed grassy borders.

Then, too, Golden Gate Park today, with its scenic beauty, its lakes and woodlands ringing with

Barney Barron, current Superintendent.

birdsong and music, serves a much wider area than it formerly did. Once a metropolitan Park serving the physical and aesthetic needs of the San Francisco citizenry, its popularity has grown to such an extent that, on weekends, the traffic well-nigh approaches gridlock. It is no more the City alone that is served, but the entire Bay Area. This creates problems of some immensity.

The present Superintendent, Mr. Barney Barron, informs me that senescence is also a major concern. Trees planted by McLaren long years ago have now grown old and must be replaced. Reforestation is expensive and the scarcity of trained gardeners renders replacement slow and difficult. The irrigation system, especially in the eastern half of the Park, is inadequate and antiquated and should be renewed and much of the greenery, lush, succulent, and luxuriant in McLaren's day, is now sparse and sere and in a sorry state—again, primarily because of the shortage of qualified maintenance crews. This is particularly true of the Arizona Garden and DeLaveaga Dell.

The problems and difficulties are legion and one can only hope and pray that each succeeding Superintendent will be given the financial wherewithal, the necessary manpower, and the loyal support of the citizenry (which is also important and essential) in order that Golden Gate Park might continue to be the world-famous, sight-seeing paradise it has become. One would also hope and pray that there will be allowed no surreptitious filching of its woods or lakes or sweeping meadows to crate yet another "concrete jungle." With these everyone is heart-sick and weary—except, of course, their builders.

Bibliography

Gardening in California: Landscape and Flower; published by A.M. Robertson; 1908.

David Cairns, S.C.M. Press; London, 1950.

The Royal Botanic Garden, Edinburgh, 1670-1970, Published by H. M. Stationery Office; Edinburgh, 1970.

Gertrude Atherton, *My San Francisco,* Bobbs-Merrill Co.

Clary, Raymond H., *The Making of Golden Gate Park, The Early Years:* Don't Call It Frisco Press; San Francisco, 1986.

Clary, Raymond H., *The Making of Golden Gate Park, The Growing Years:* Don't Call It Frisco Press; San Francisco, 1987.

Index

About the Author

Tom Girvan Aikman, McLaren's grandnephew, was born in Bannockburn, Scotland, the son of a Scottish farmer. After high school education at Morrison's Boys School, Crieff, Perthshire, he enlisted, during World War Two, in H.M. Royal Marines and saw action during the Normandy landings. He was a parachutist. After the war he entered St. Andrews University from which he graduated Master of Arts in 1948. A classicist, he next pursued theology with a view to offering for the Christian ministry. Ordained by the Church of Scotland, he has served congregations in Southern Rhodesia (Zimbabwe), Scotland, England, and America. The possessor of an earned doctoral degree (International Seminary) for a thesis on the Medieval Synthesis, he has served a busy and active Presbyterian Church in upstate New York for the past sixteen years.

His Welsh wife is a Presbyterian minister's daughter, a graduate of the University of Durham, England, and a descendant of the illustrious Welsh Revivalist preacher, the Rev. Daniel Rowland, whose statue stands in Llangeitho, Cardiganshire and of General Sir Thomas Picton who fought at Waterloo and whose memorial stands in the North Transept of St. Paul's Cathedral, London.